Keyword Cards

This booklet contains 100 tear-out cards, with three illustrated Keywords for each letter sound introduced in *Fix-it Phonics Level One*.

You can use the cards to introduce the Keywords for a lesson, or consolidate vocabulary knowledge by playing games with them as detailed below.

You could review 4-8 cards at the start of each lesson, gradually increasing the speed to make sure everyone is really awake at the start of their class!

The cards have the pictogram in the top left corner, as well as the growing rainbow system in the bottom right corner, allowing you to quickly identify the Unit and organise your cards.

Activity Ideas

Who likes...? / Who likes this...?
Show a card (e.g. cake) and ask, **"Who likes cake?"**. Encourage children to respond with the name of the Letterlander who starts the word e.g. "Clever Cat likes cake".

Flash
Flash a card quickly in front of the children. Ask, **"Is this a...(e.g. cat)?"** Children respond "yes" or "no". Start off slowly to make sure the children know the words, and make sure you also include some questions where the answer is "no!".

What's missing?
Display some of the cards and ask the children to close their eyes or cover it with a towel. Then take one card away and ask, **"What's missing?"**.

Word sort
Shuffle the cards, then ask children to sort the pictures in to sets of 3 with the same initial sound, e.g. **sun**, **sea**, **sand**.

Contents

s	sun	sea	sand	r	rain	river	rice
a	apple	ant	arrow	h	hat	house	hand
t	table	toys	ten	b	book	ball	boat
p	pen	paint	pencil	f	fish	frog	fire
i	in	ink	insect	l	log	leg	lion
n	nine	nose	noodles	j	jet	juice	jam
m	map	milk	man	v	van	vegetables	vet
d	dog	drum	dad	w	water	watch	window
g	garden	gate	grass	x	six	box	fox
o	on	off	orange	y	yo-yo	yellow	yogurt
c	car	cup	cake	z	zero	zip	zoo
k	key	kettle	kitchen	q	quarter	question	quilt
ck	kick	sack	sock	ng	sing	king	ring
e	egg	envelope	elbow	a	apron	alien	acorn
u	up	under	umbrella	e	eat	east	eagle
				i	ice cream	island	iron
				o	open	old	ocean
				u	uniform	unicycle	unicorn

 For a downloadable version of this resource, visit:
www.letterland.com/teacher-resources

© Letterland International 2018
Reprinted 2021.
10 9 8 7 6 5 4 3

ISBN: 978-1-78248-289-5
Product Code: TK12

Published by Letterland International Ltd. 8/10 South Street, Epsom, Surrey, KT18 7PF, UK
www.letterland.com
LETTERLAND™ is a trademark of Letterland International Ltd.

Written by: Lisa Holt
Design by: Lisa Holt and Laura Bittles

Originator of Letterland: Lyn Wendon

The author asserts the moral right to be identified as the author of this work.
All rights reserved. No part of this publication may be reproduced, stored in a retrieval system, or transmitted in any form or by any means, electronic, mechanical, photocopying, recording or otherwise, without either the prior permission of the Publisher or a licence permitting restricted copying in the United Kingdom issued by the Copyright Licensing Agency Ltd, 90 Tottenham Court Road, London W1T 4LP. This book is sold subject to the condition that it shall not by way of trade or otherwise be lent, hired out or otherwise circulated without the Publisher's prior consent.

Printed in China.

s

s

s

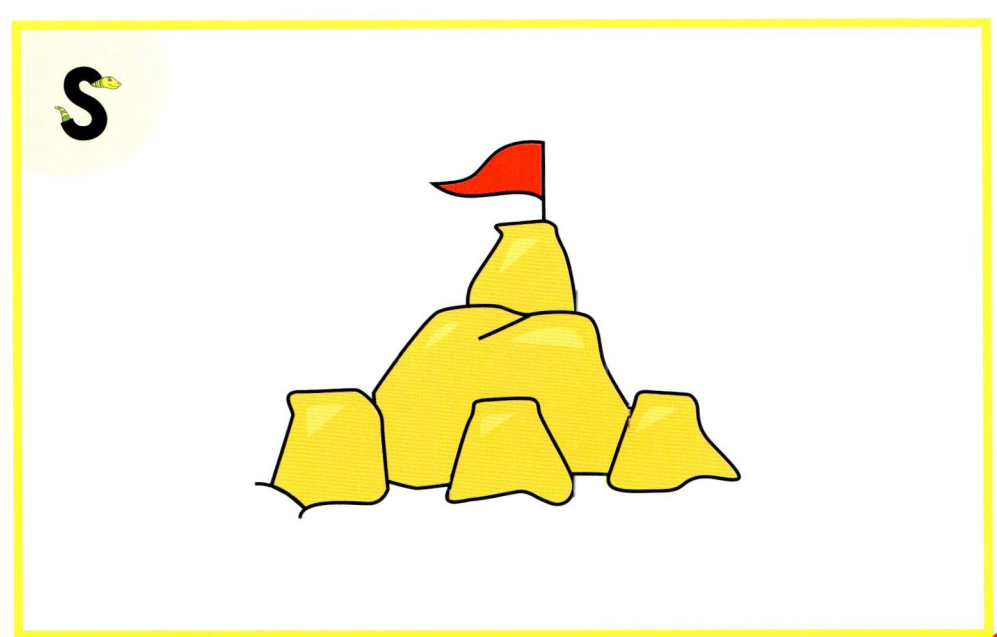

a

sand	**a**nt
sun	**s**ea

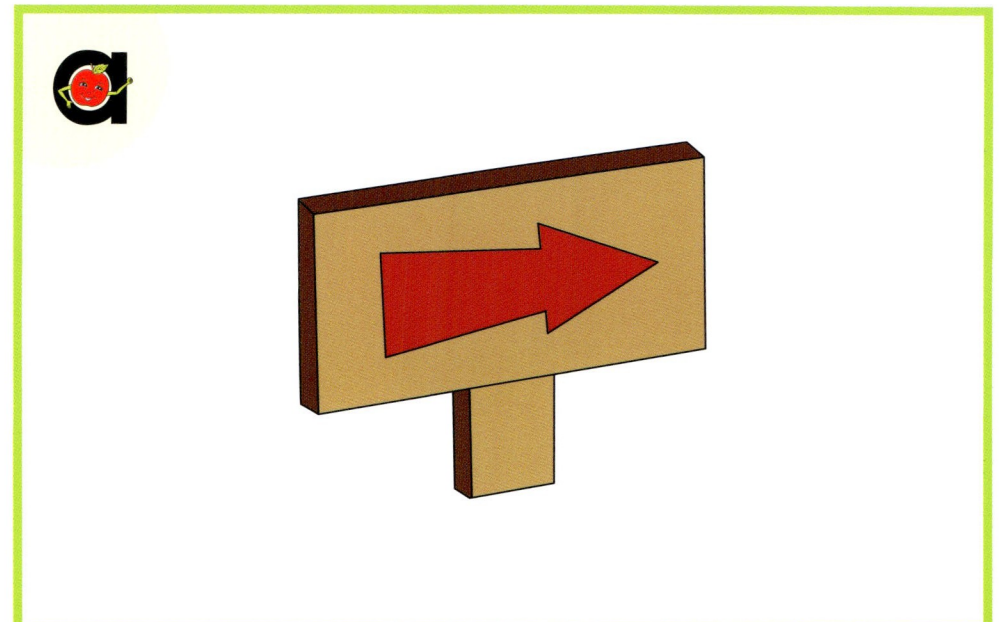

toys

table

arrow

apple

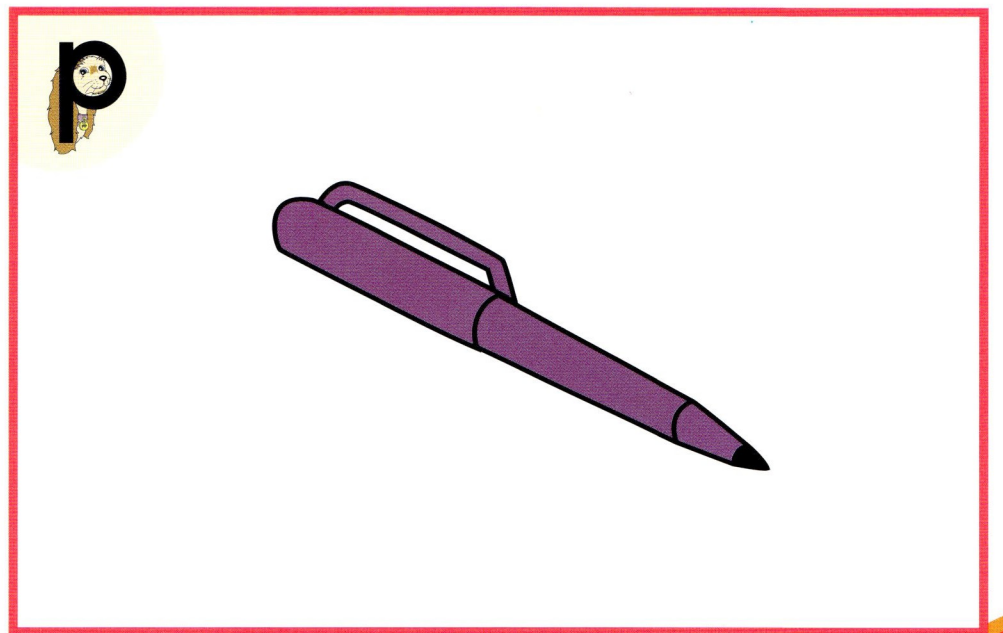
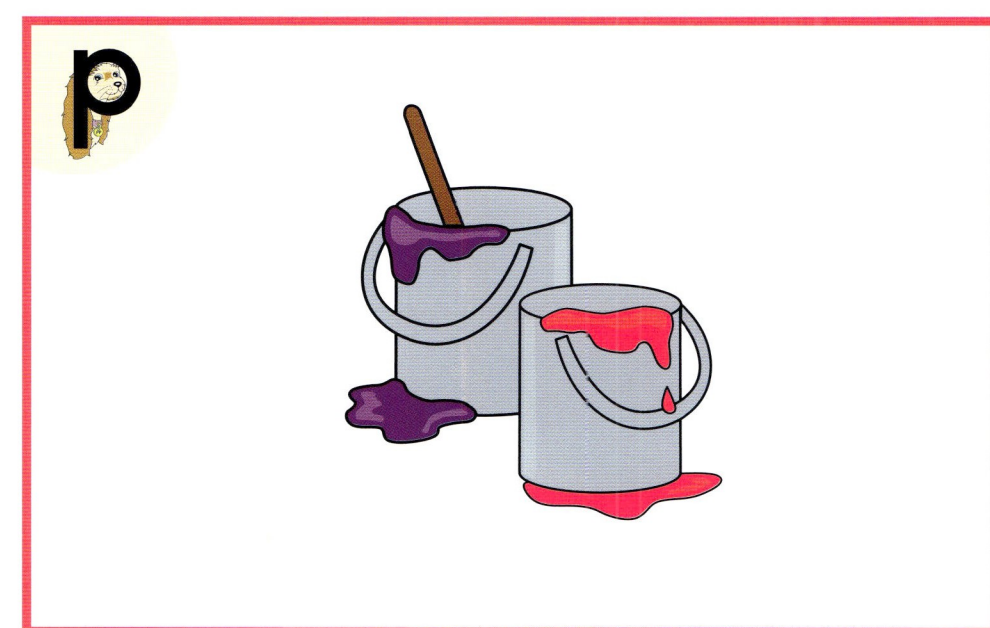

 pen

 ten

 pencil

 paint

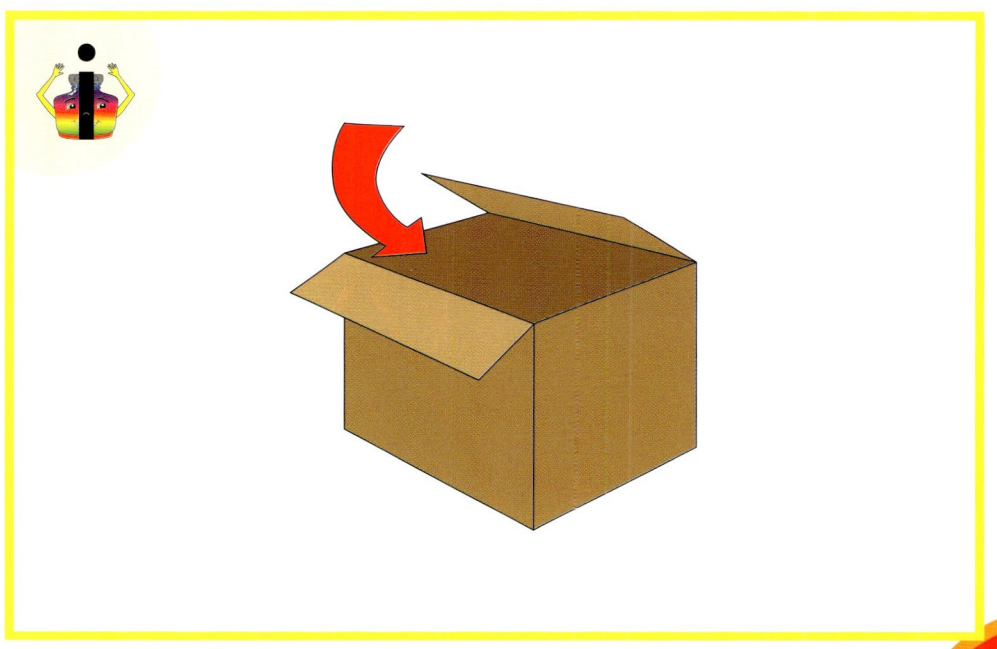

 ink

 in

 nine

 insect

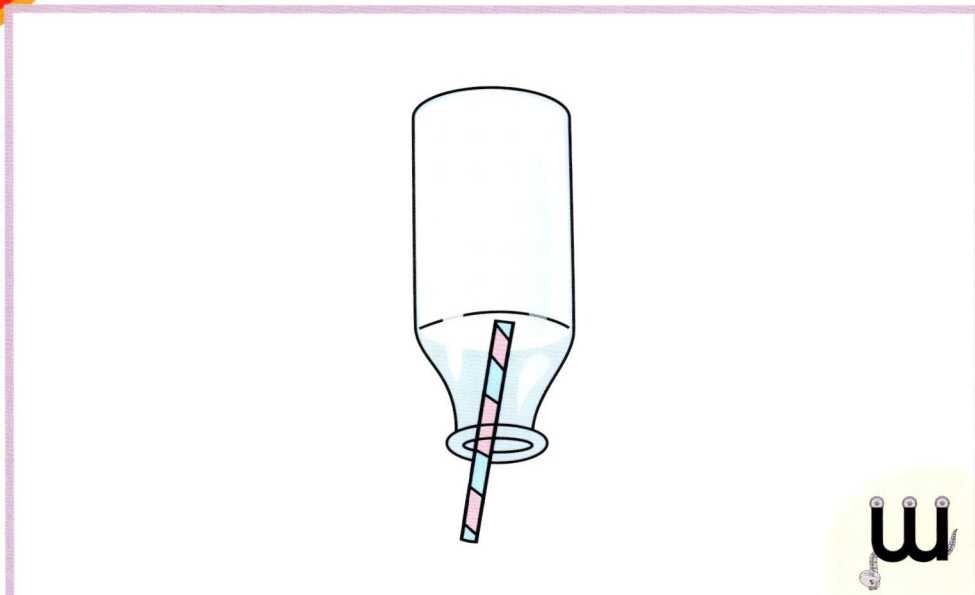

m

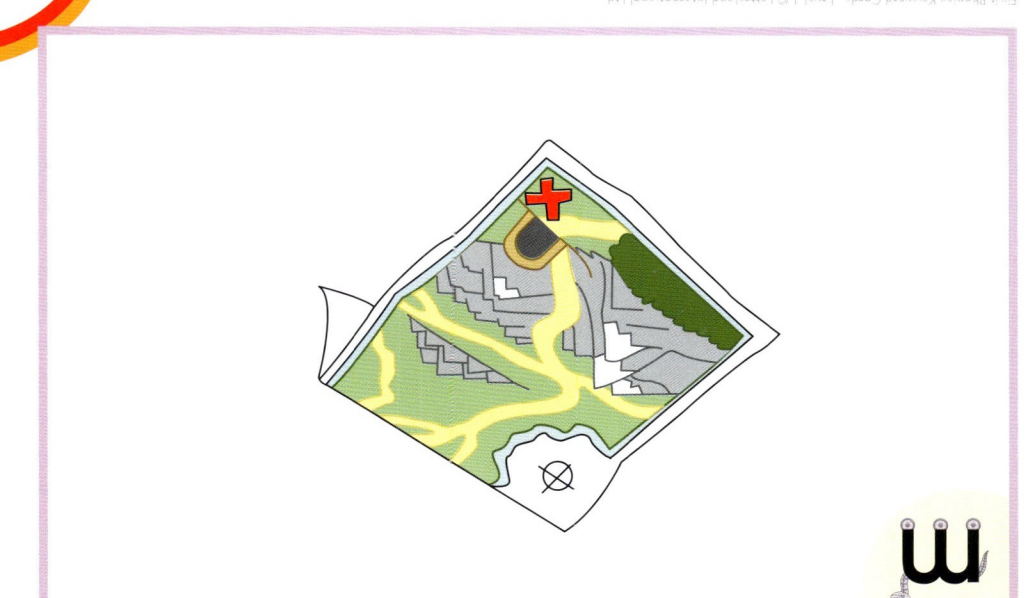

m

u

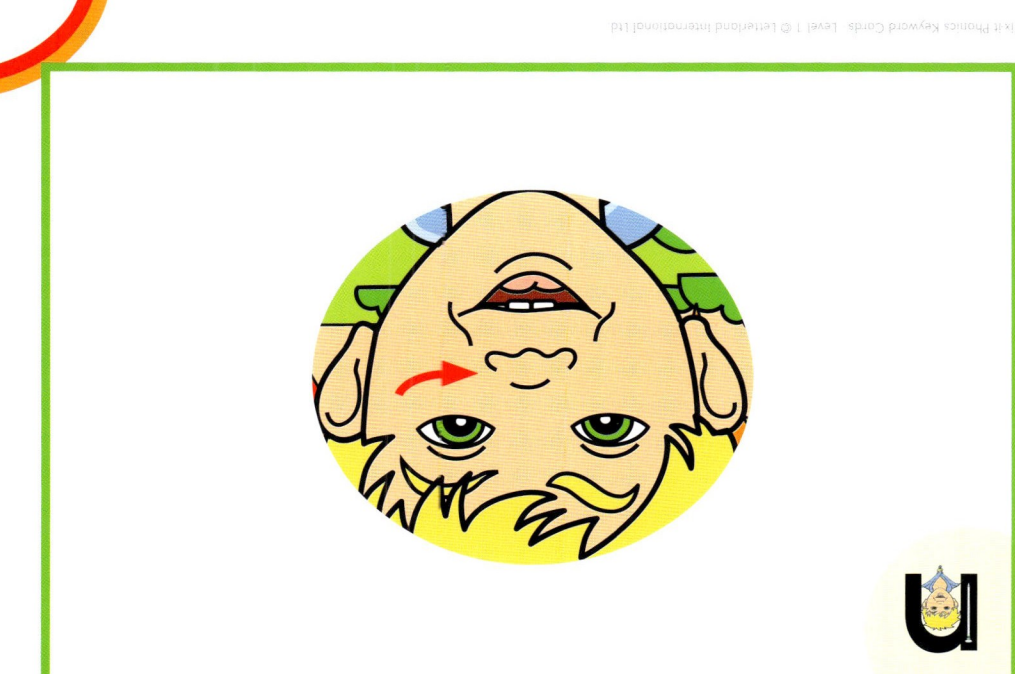

u

 noodles

 nose

 milk

 man

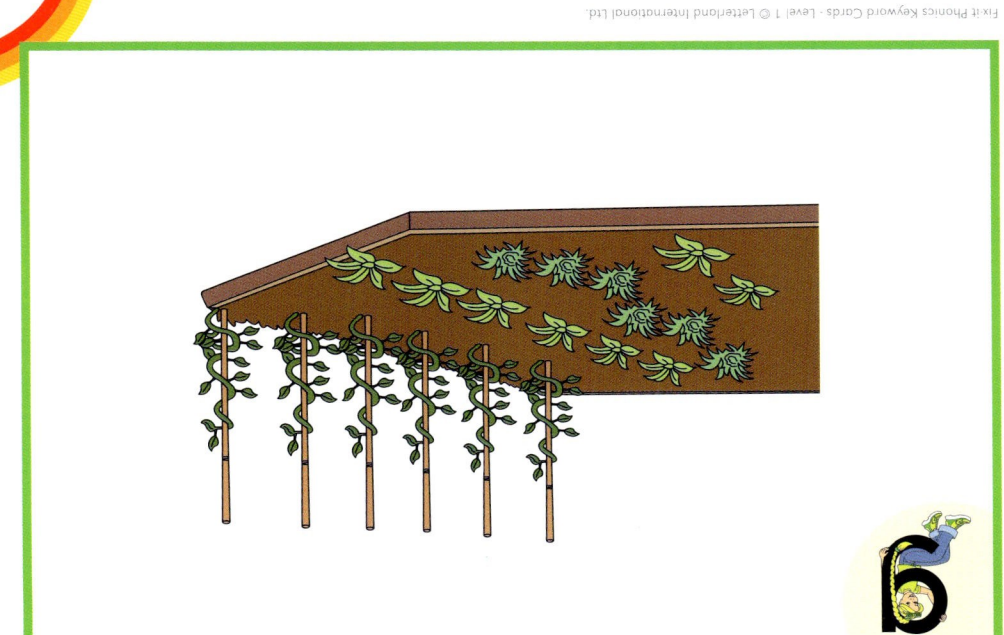

 drum

 dog

 garden

 dad

 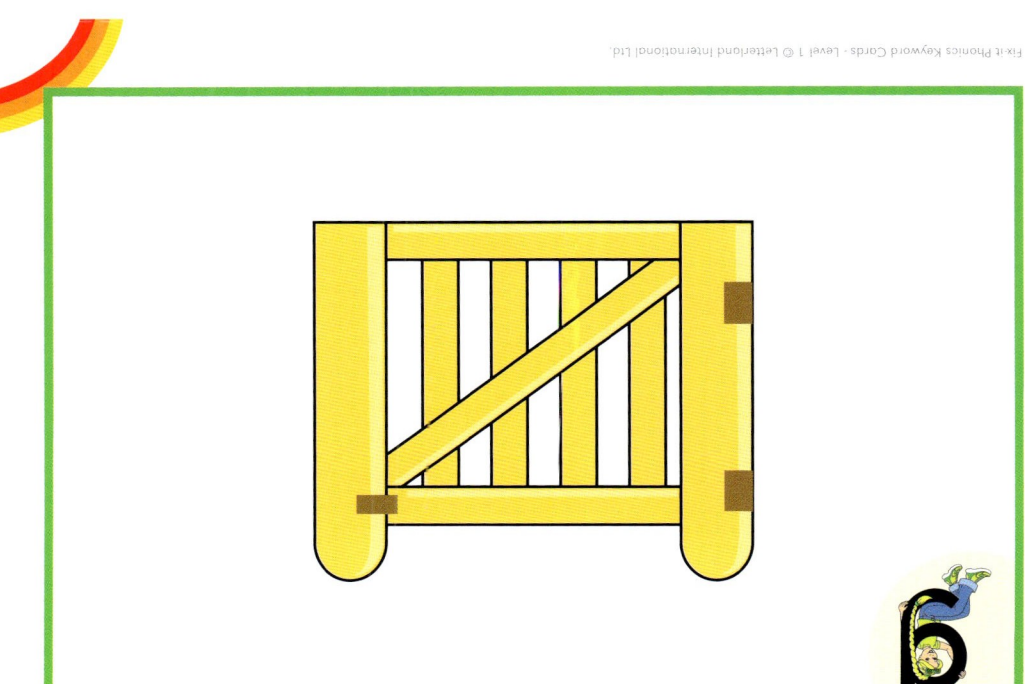

 grass

 gate

 orange

 on

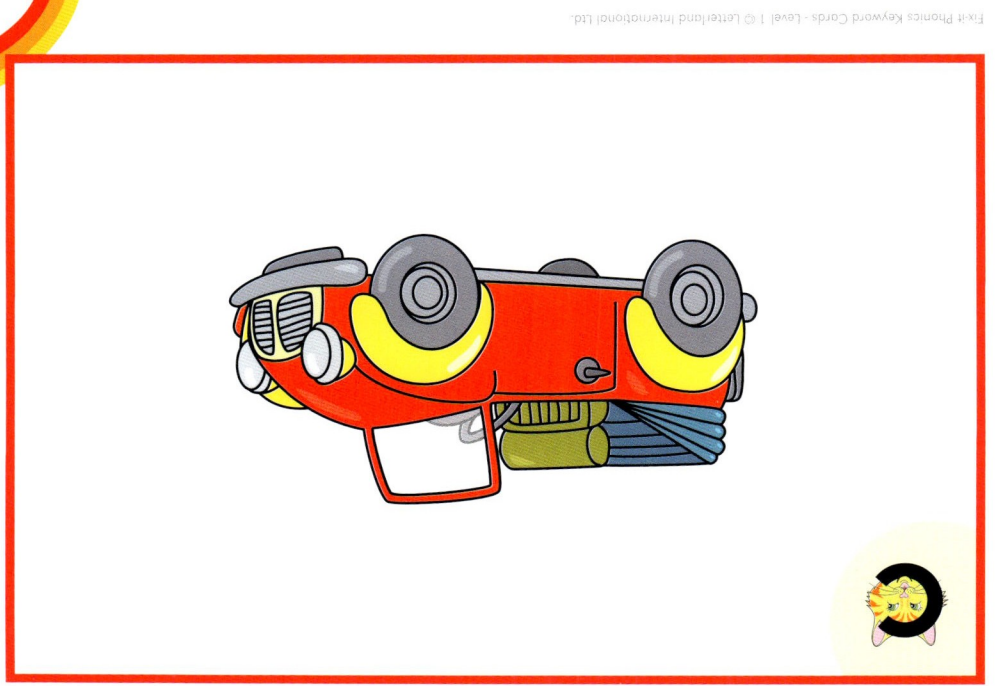

car

off

cake

cup

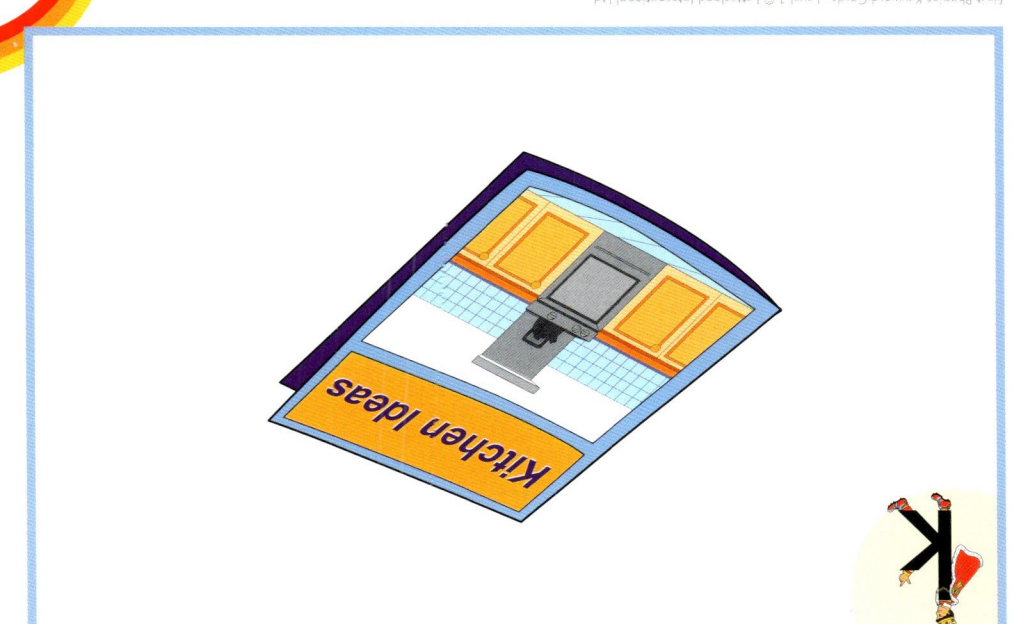

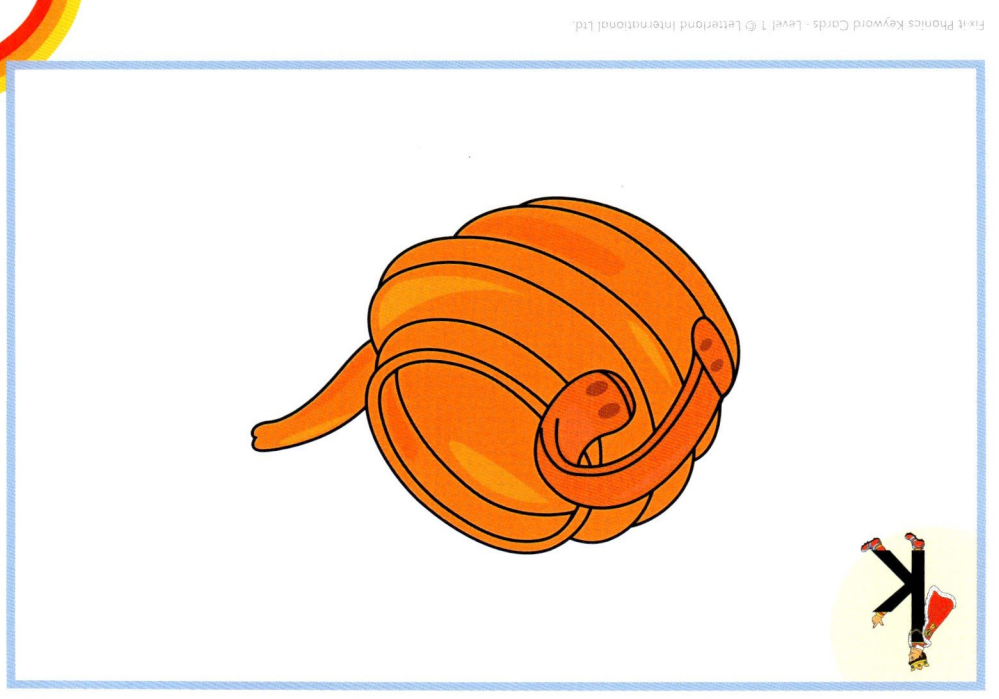

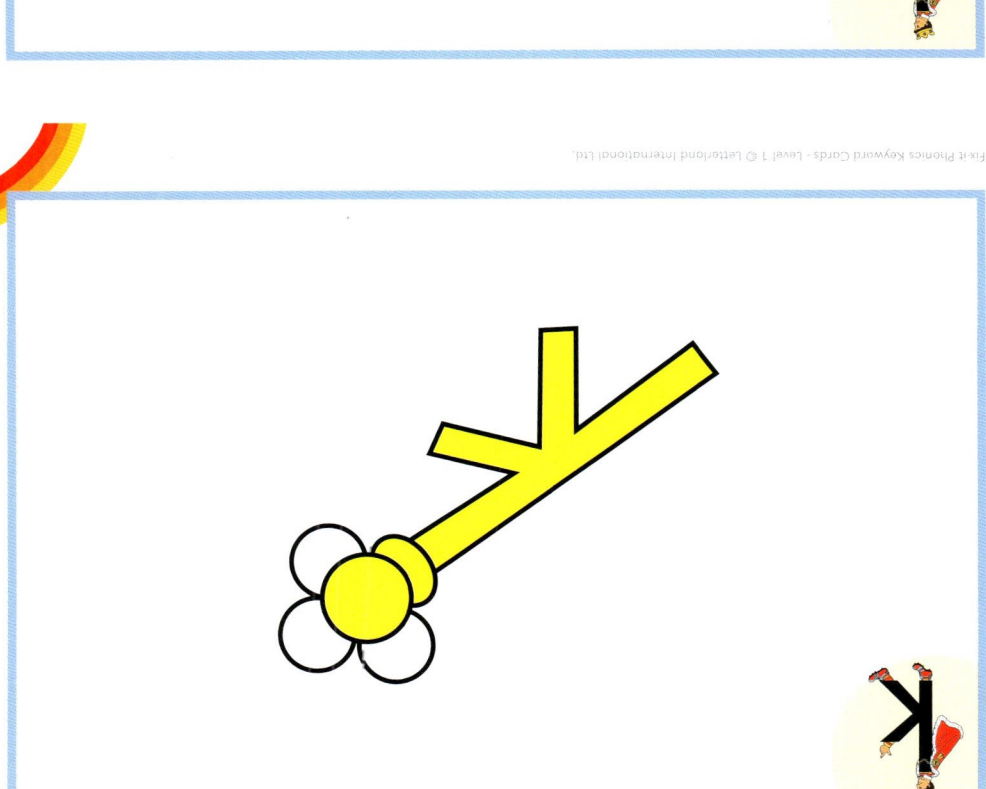

 kettle

 key

 kick

 kitchen

 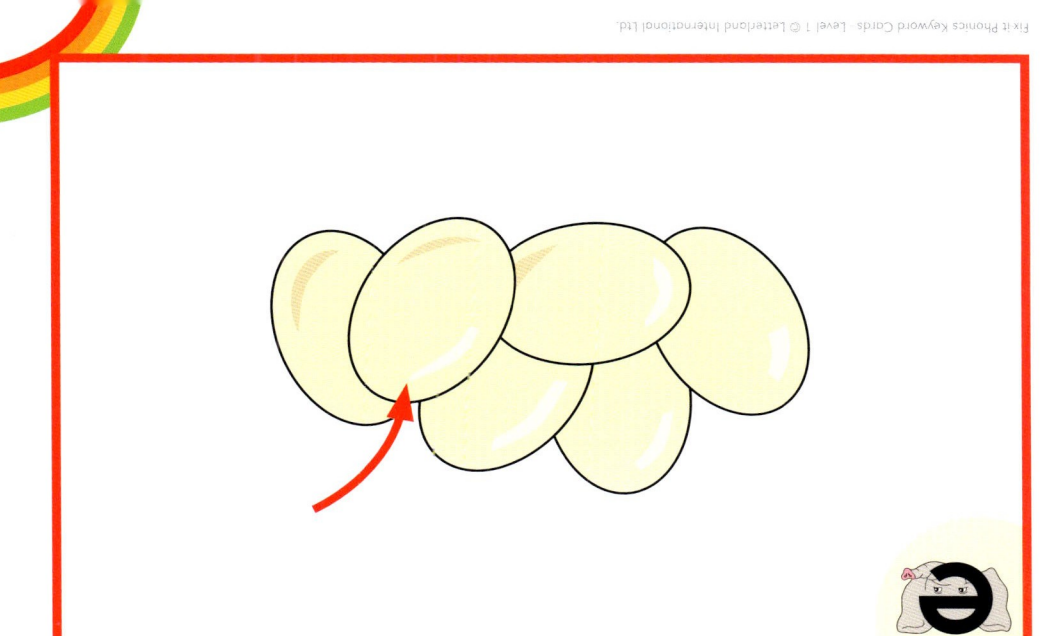

 sock

 sack

 envelope

 egg

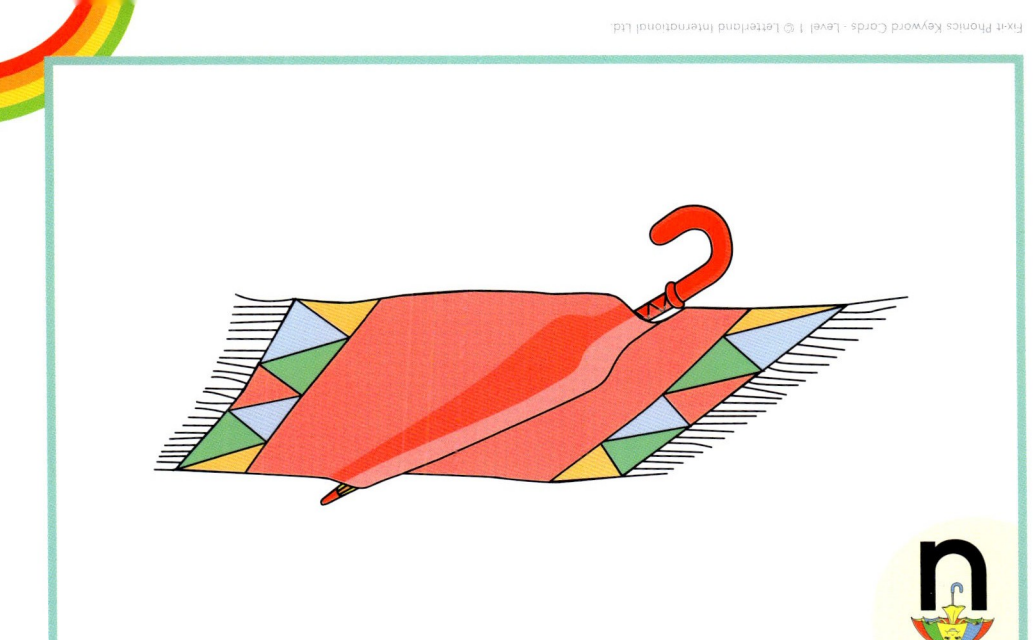
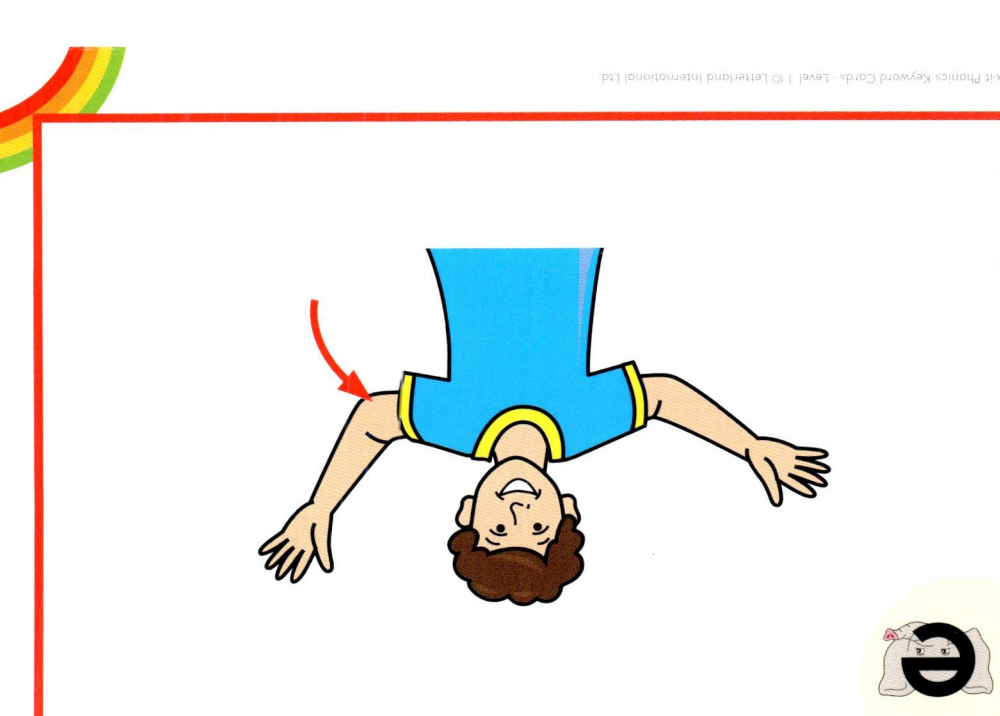

 up

 elbow

 umbrella

 under

Make your own card

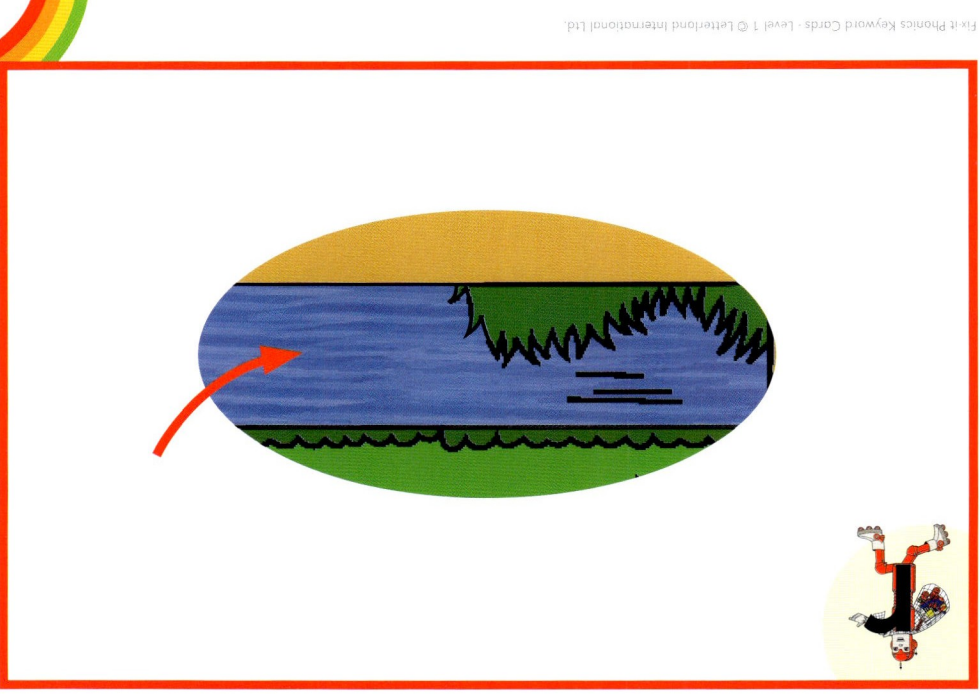

river

rain

Make your own card

rice

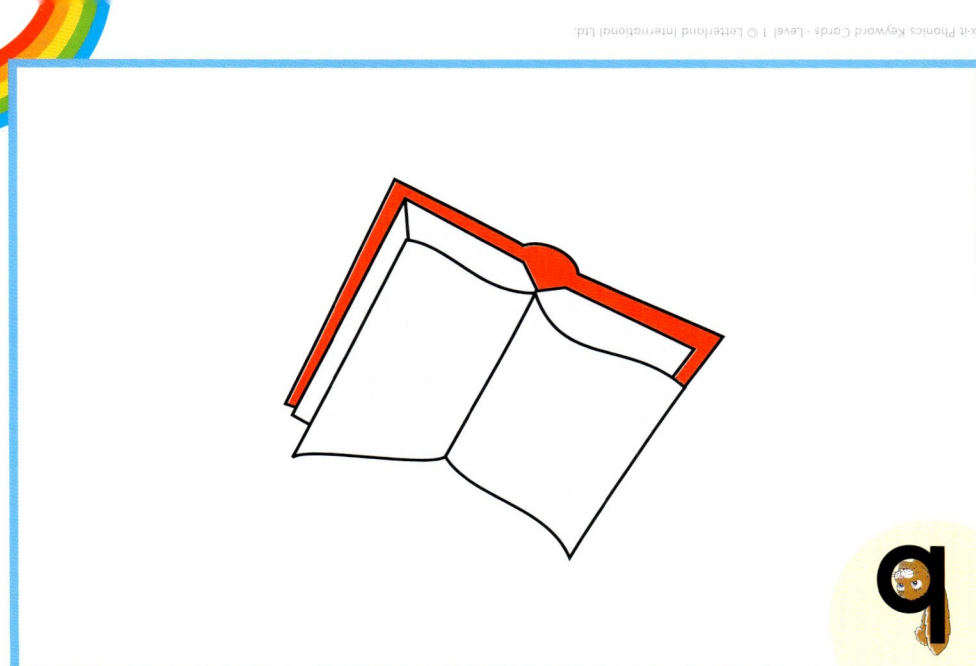

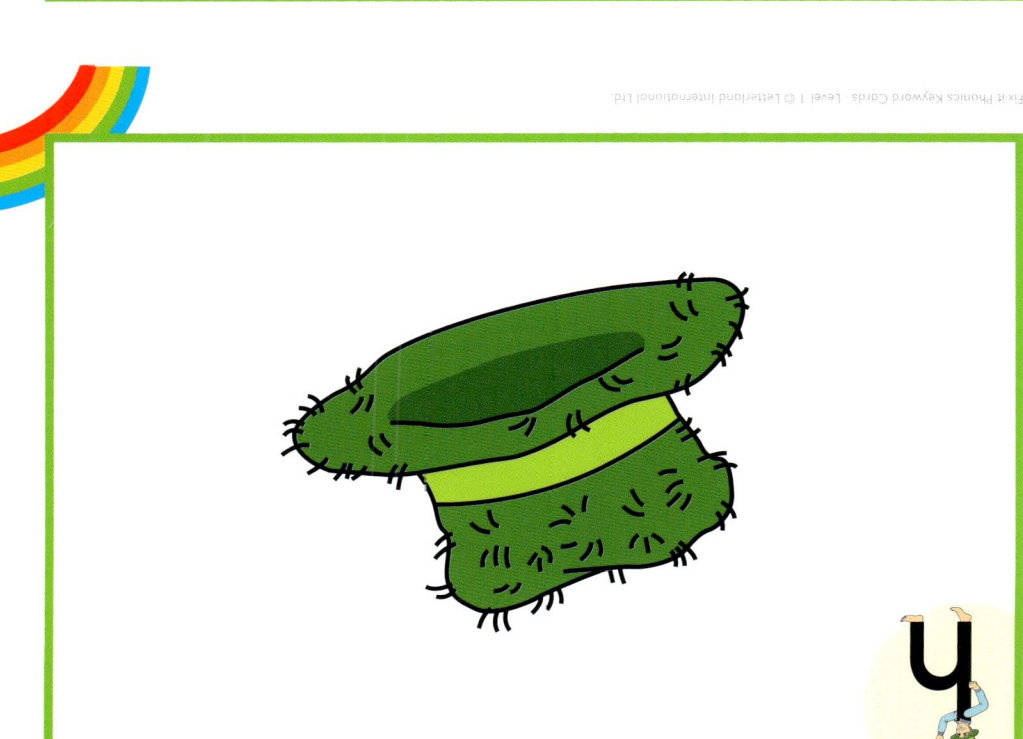

 hand

 hat

 book

 house

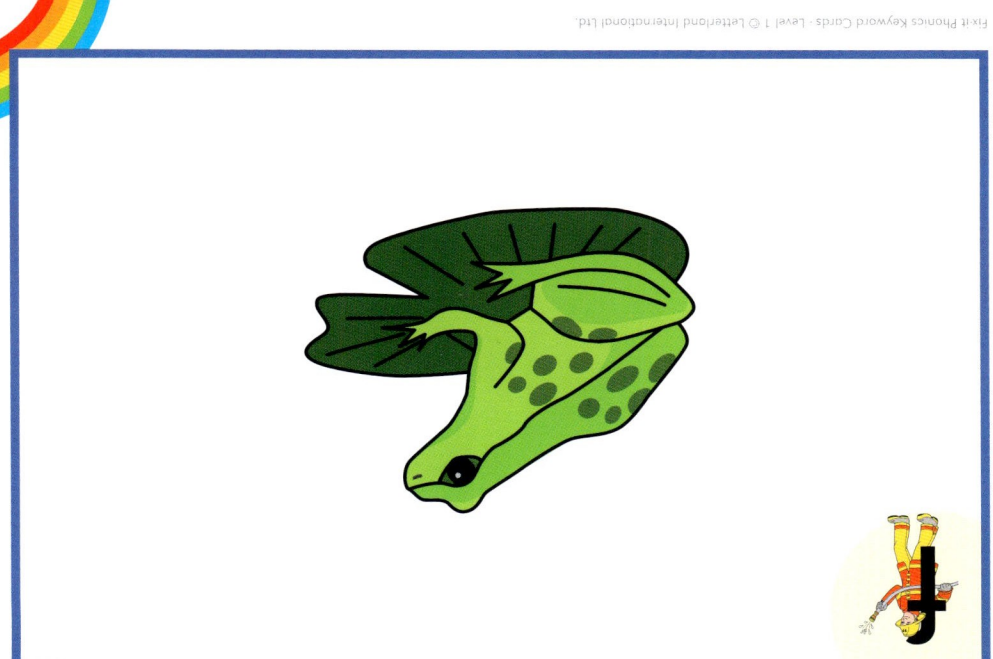
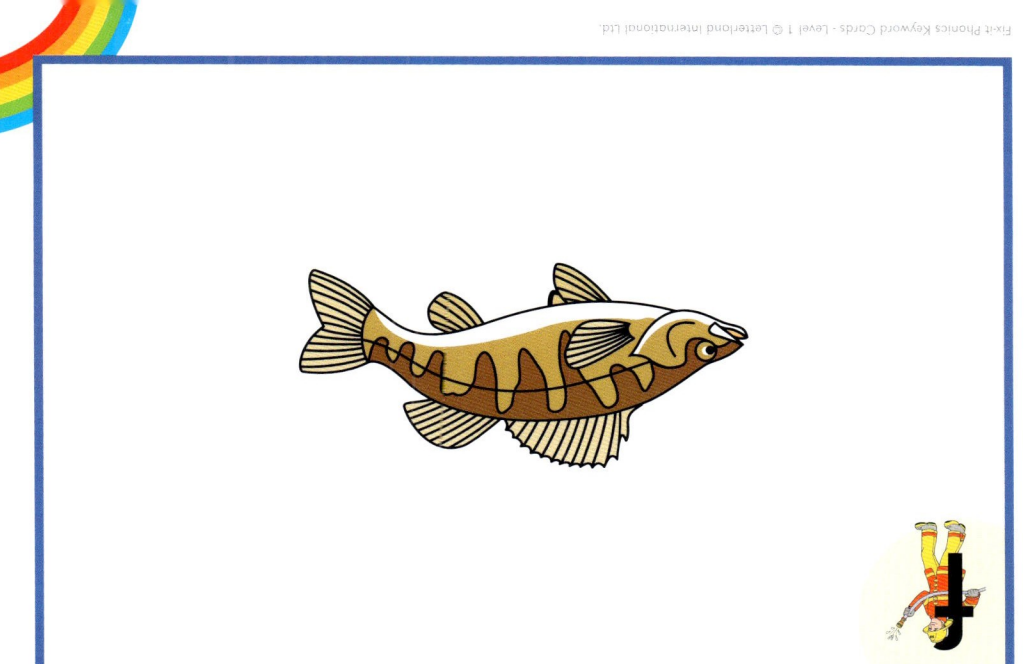
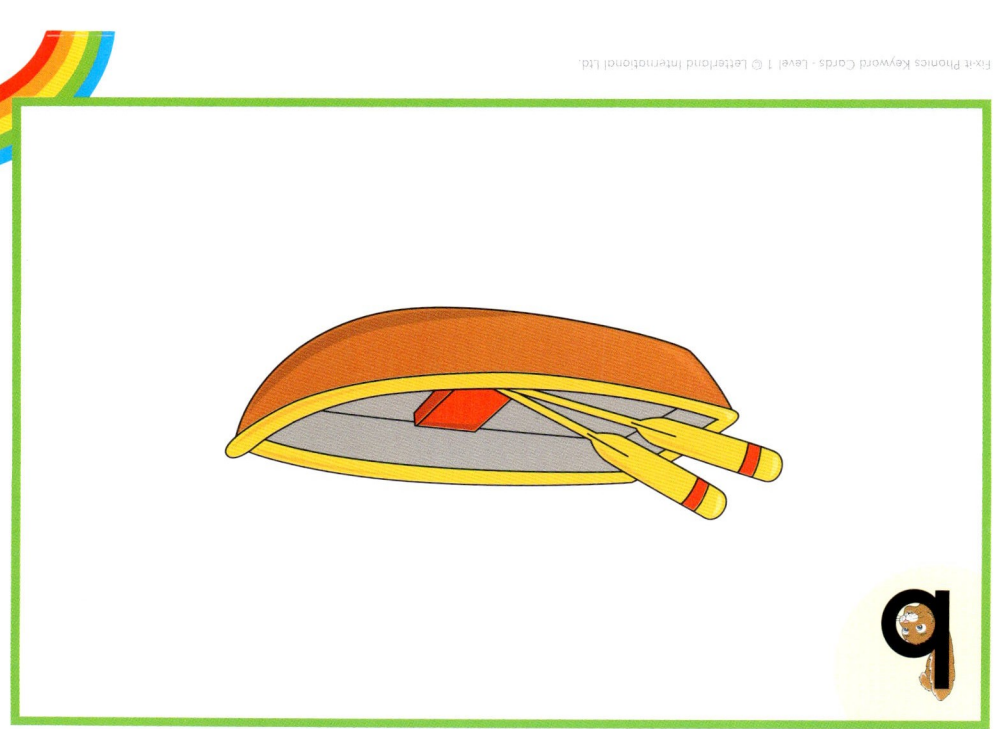
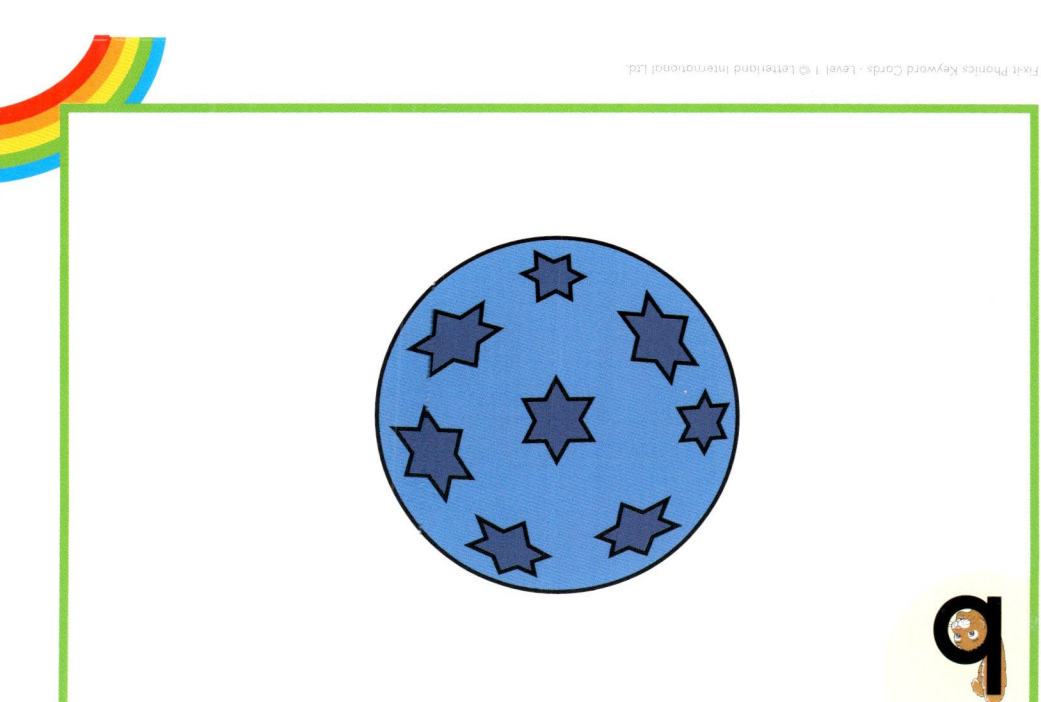

 boat

 ball

 frog

 fish

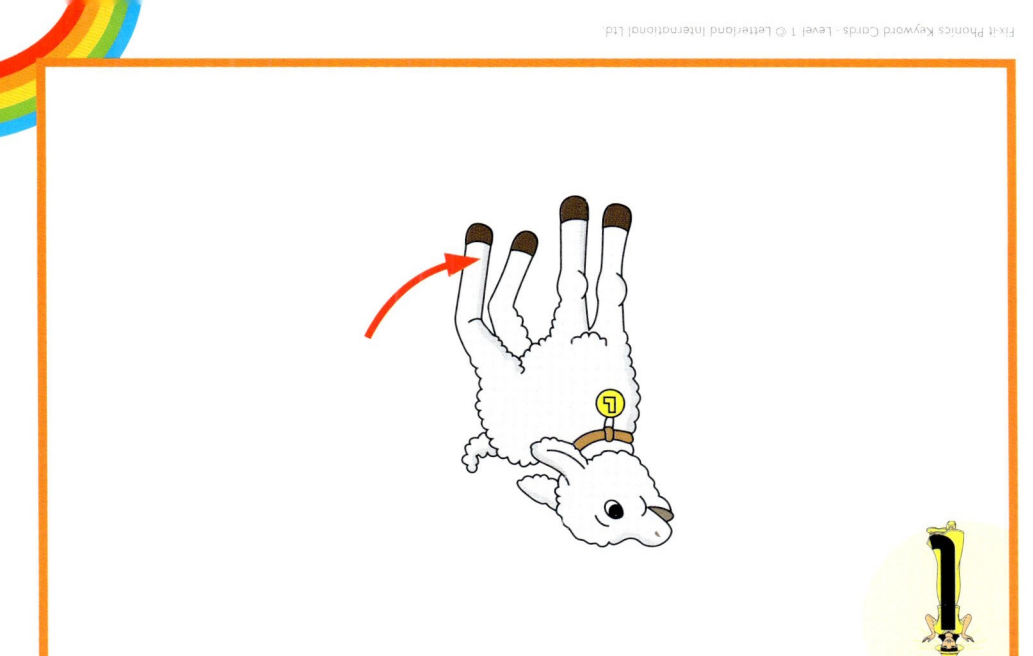

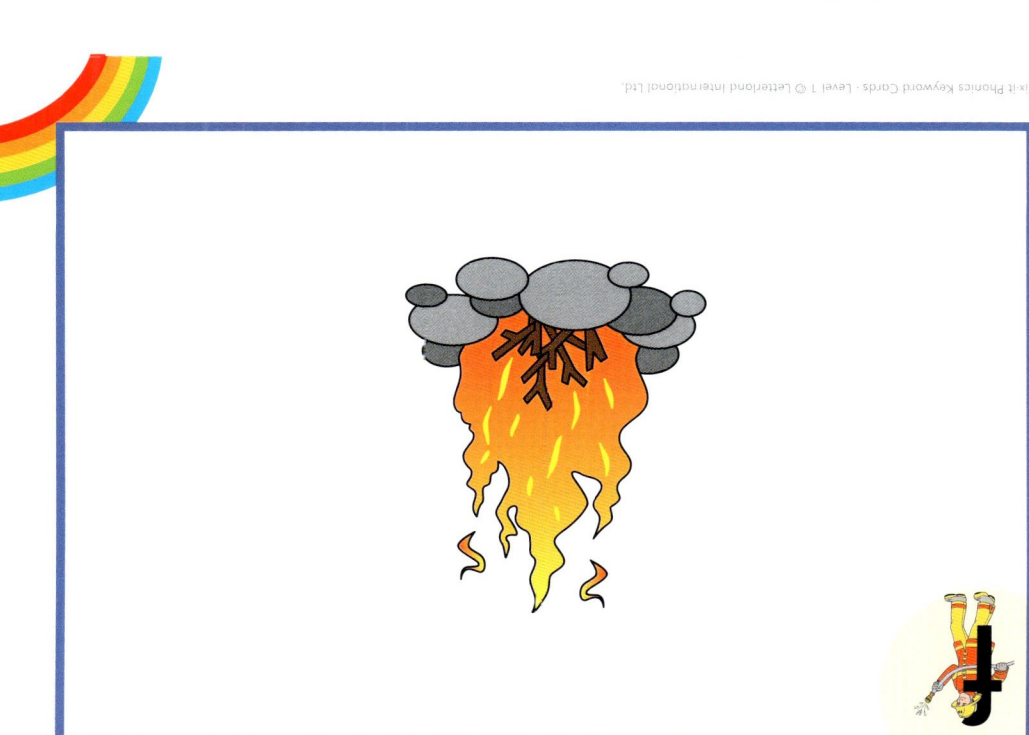

 log

 fire

 lion

 lamb

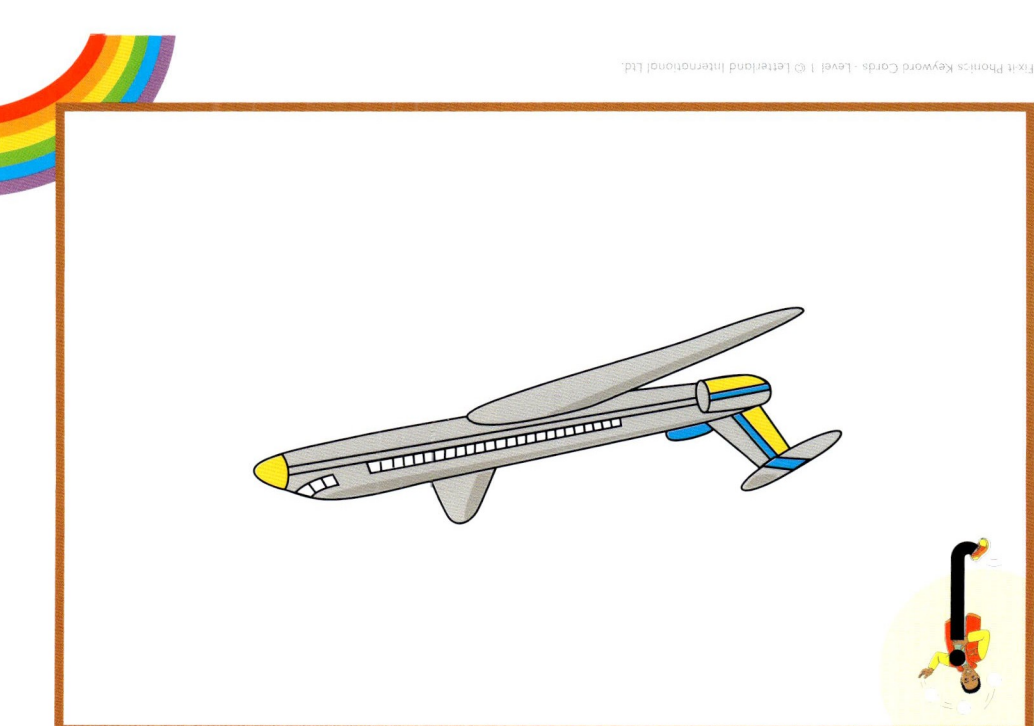

 juice

 jet

 van

 jam

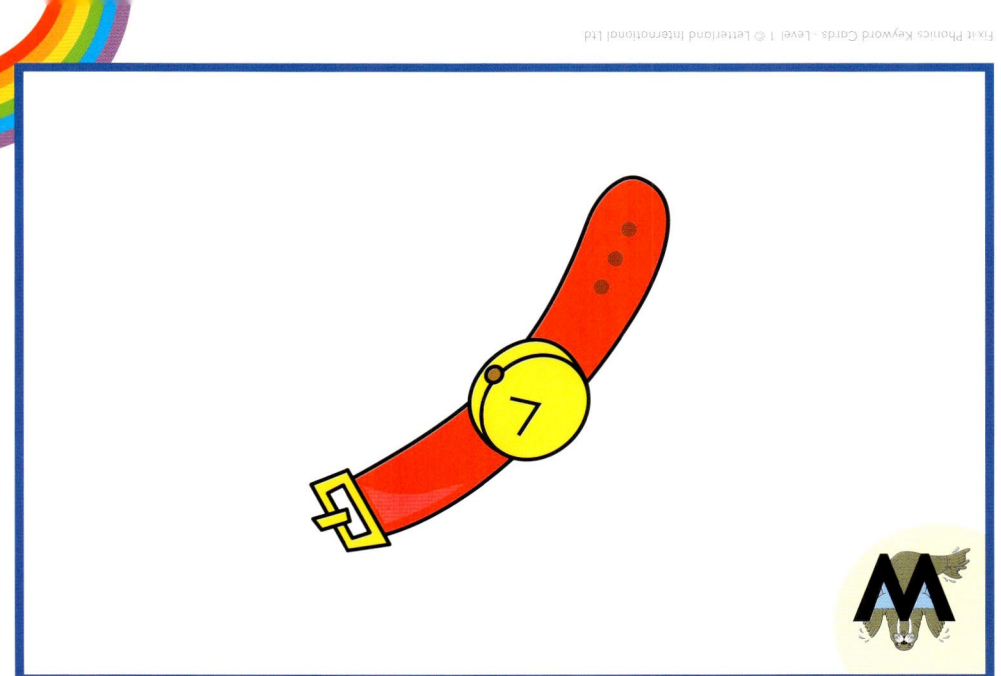
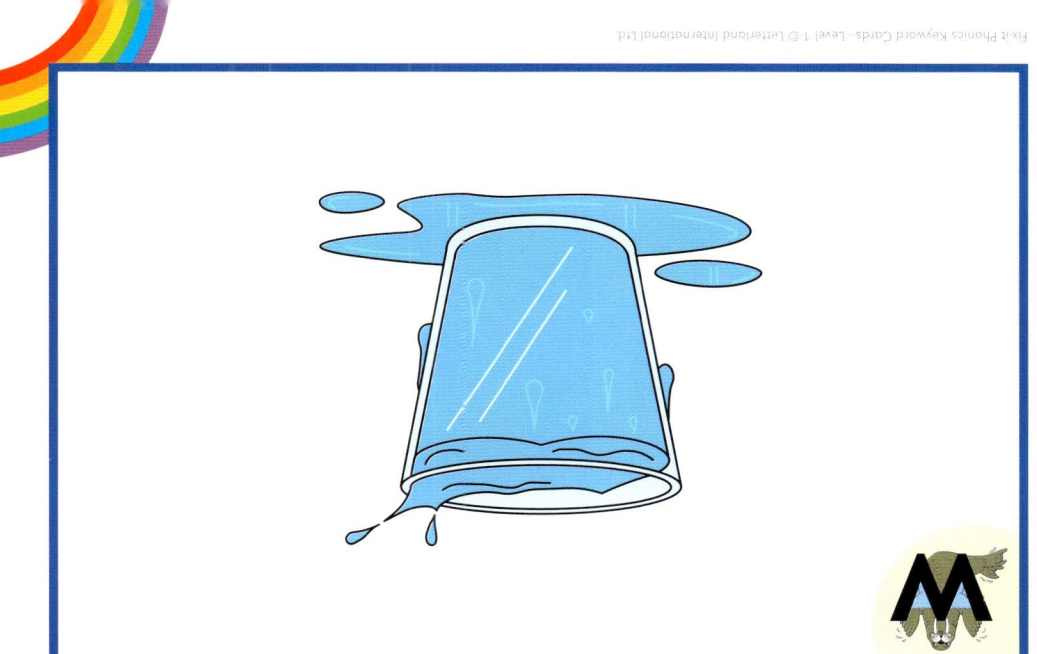
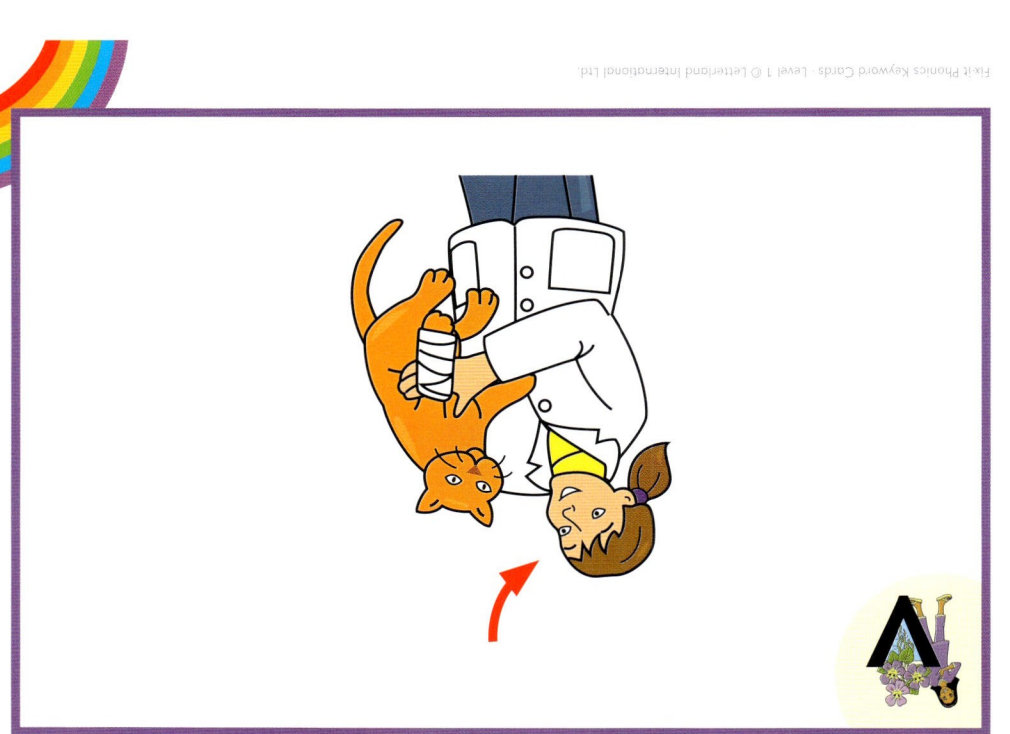
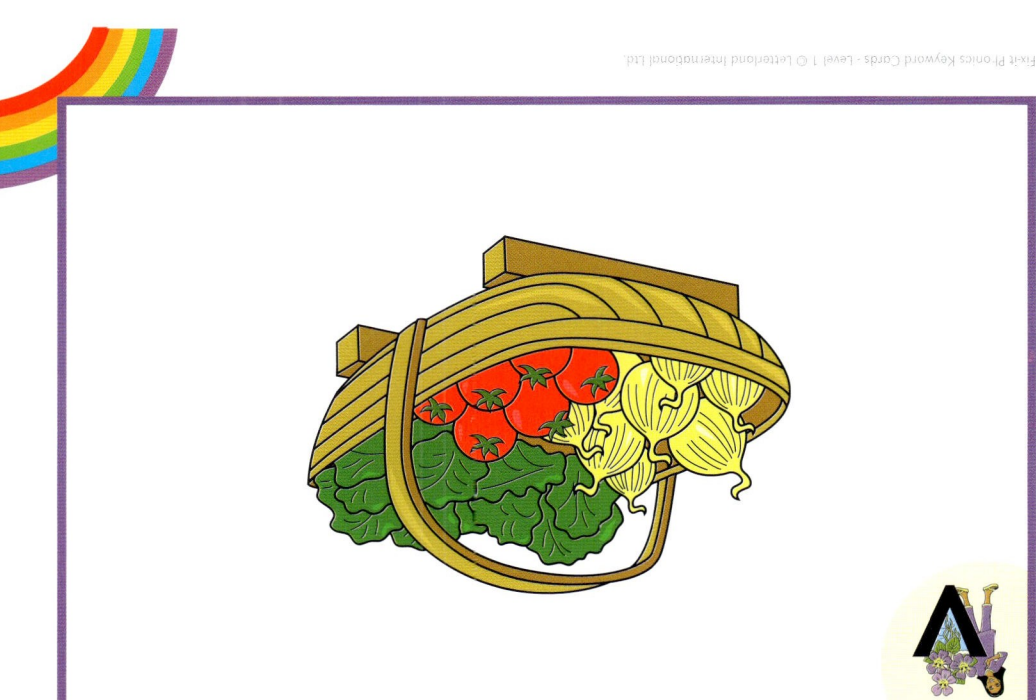

 vet

 vegetables

 watch

 water

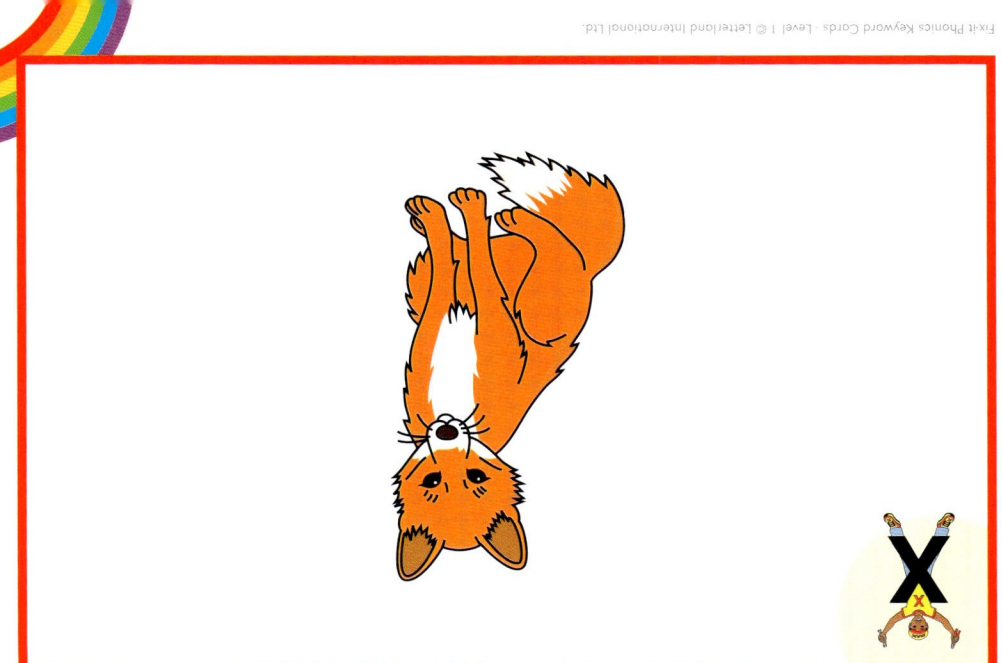
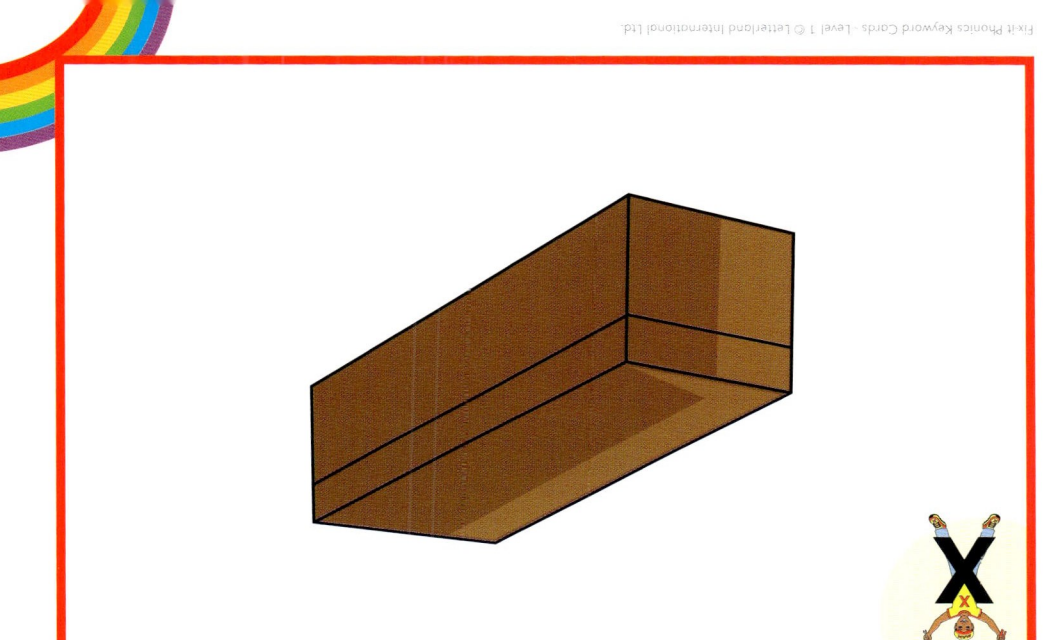
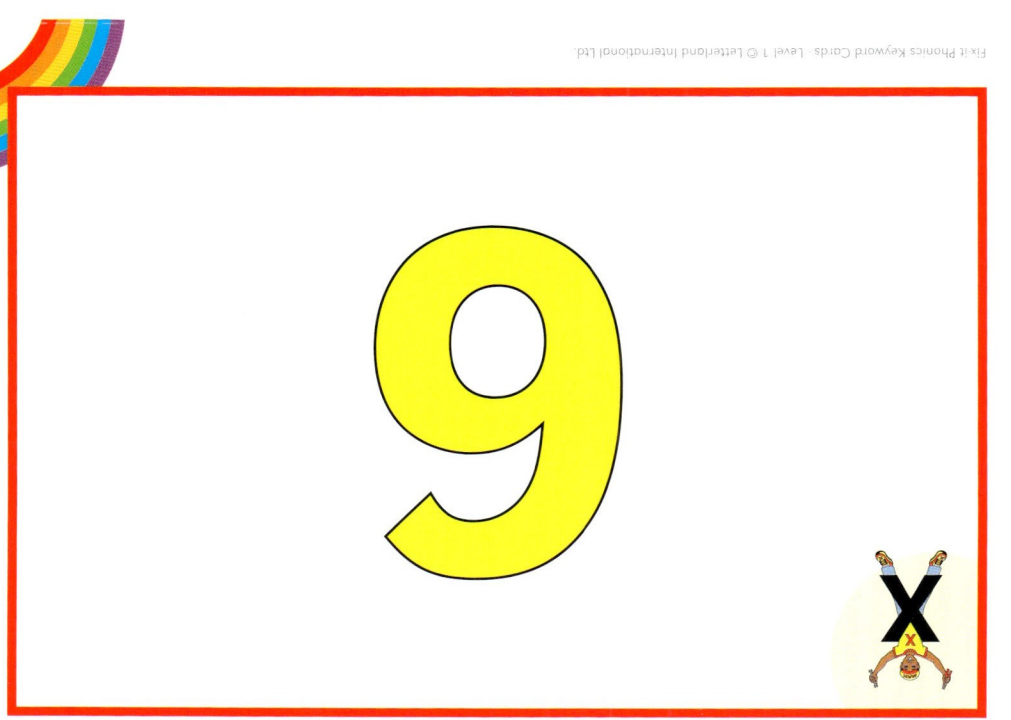
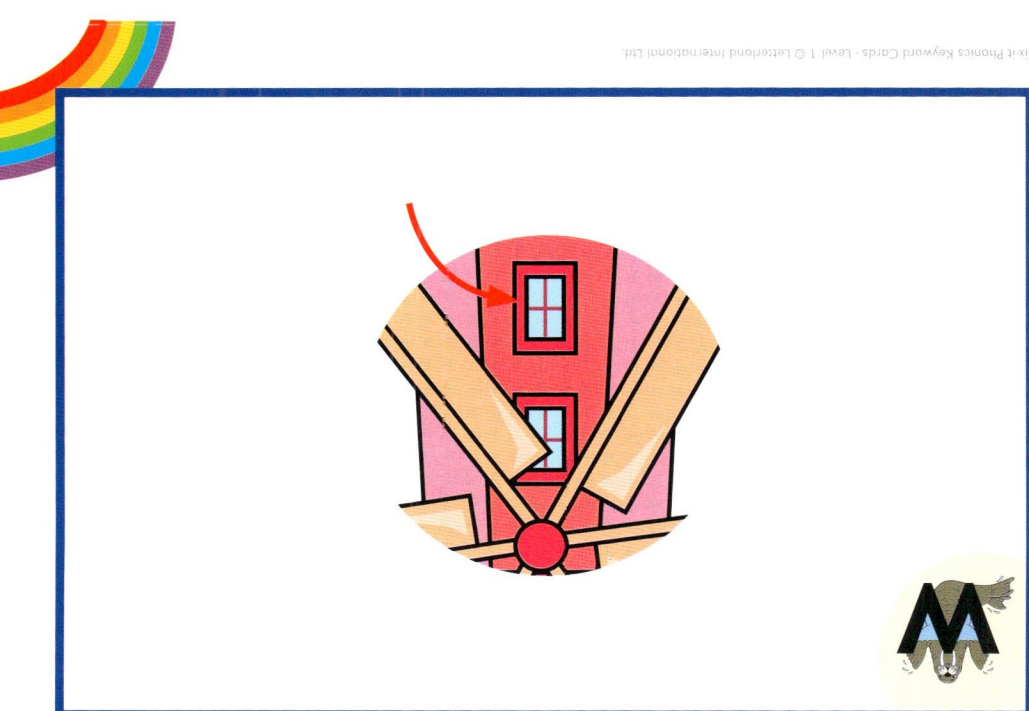

six

window

fox

box

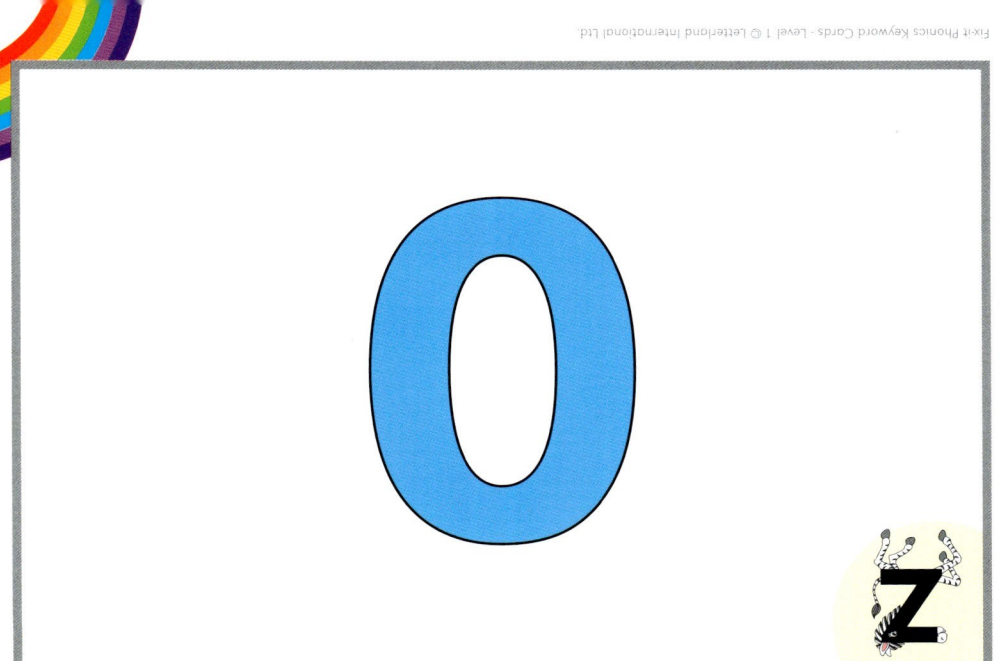

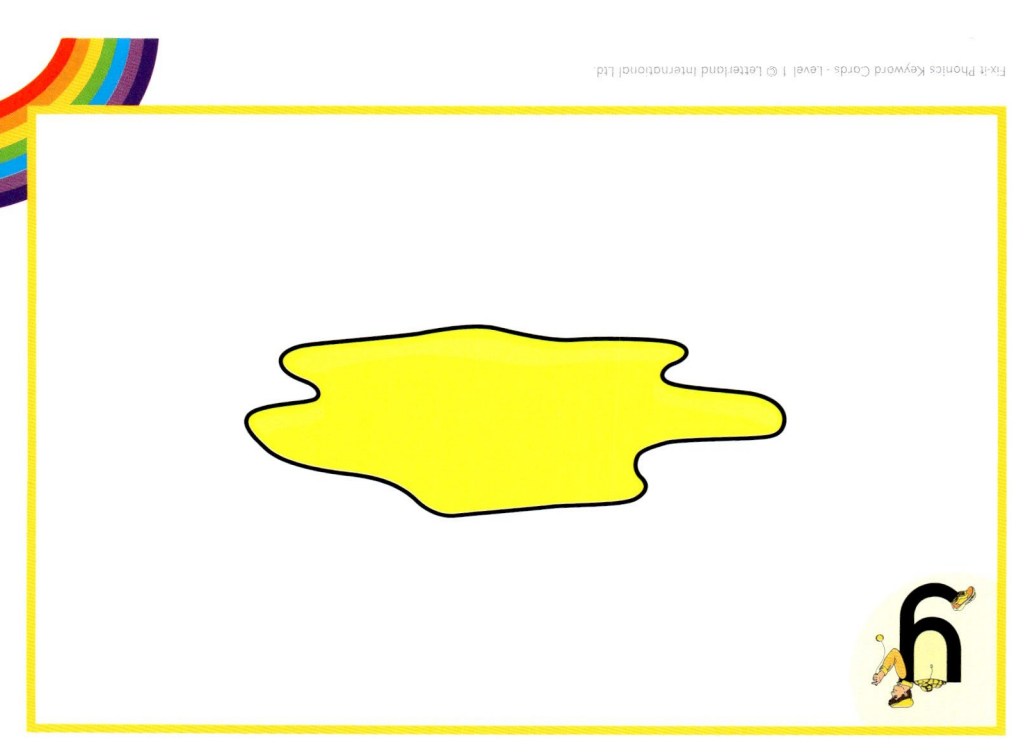
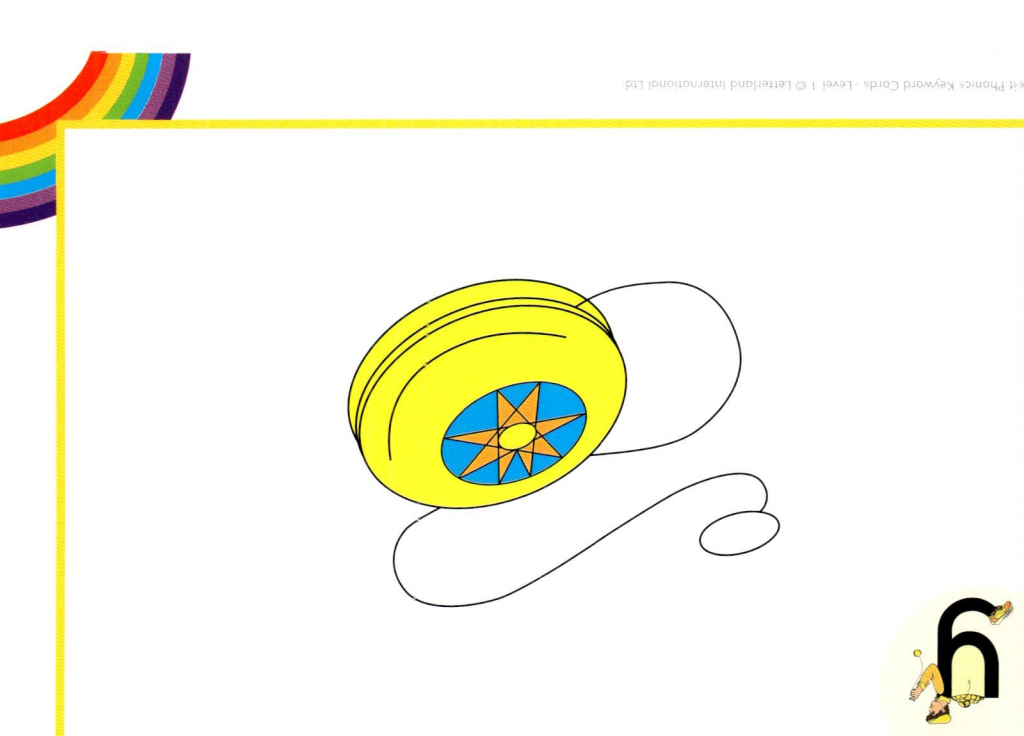

yellow

yo-yo

zero

yogurt

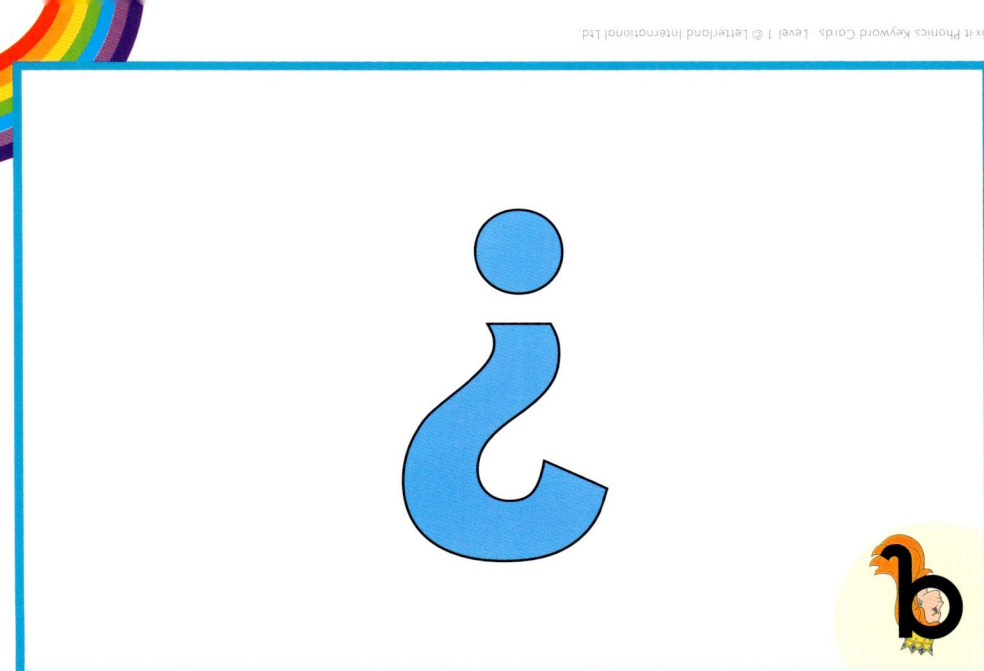
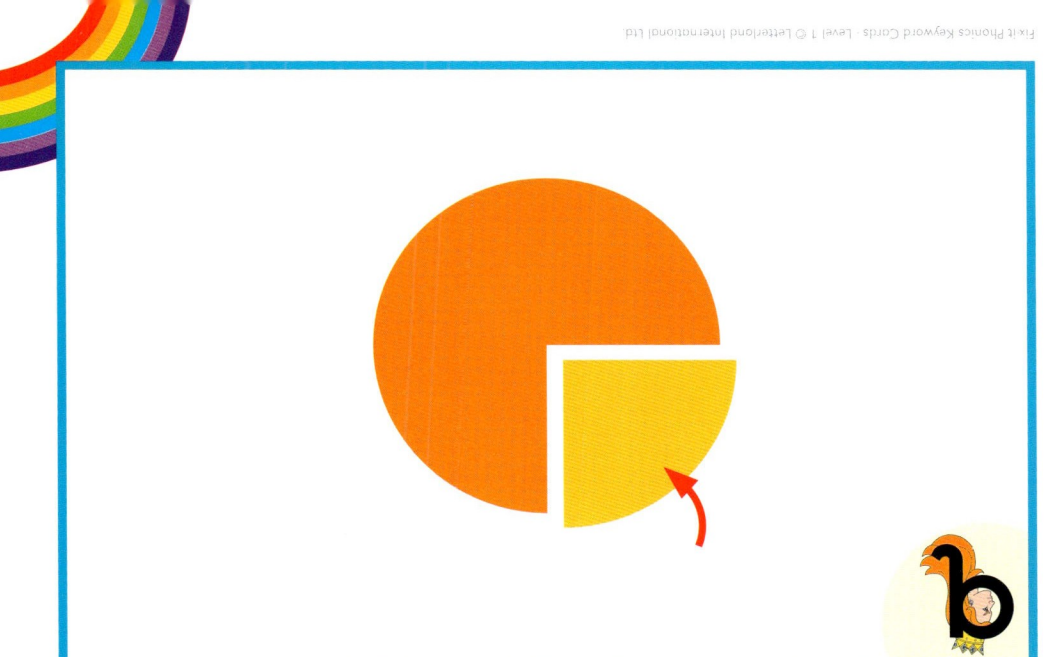

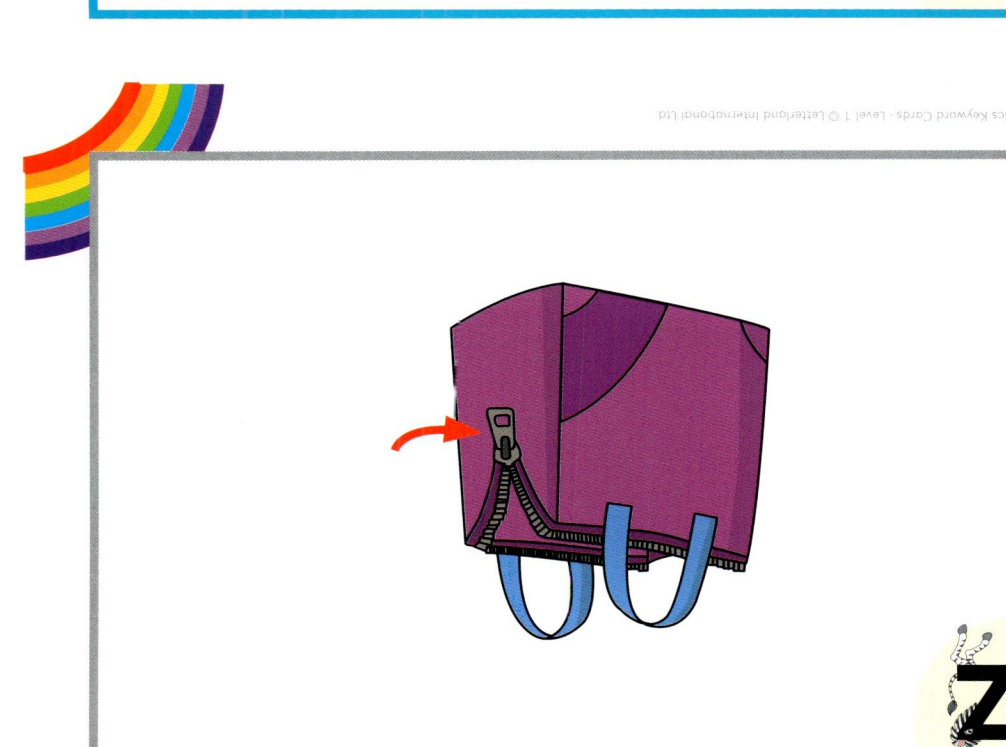

 zoo

 zip

 question

 quarter

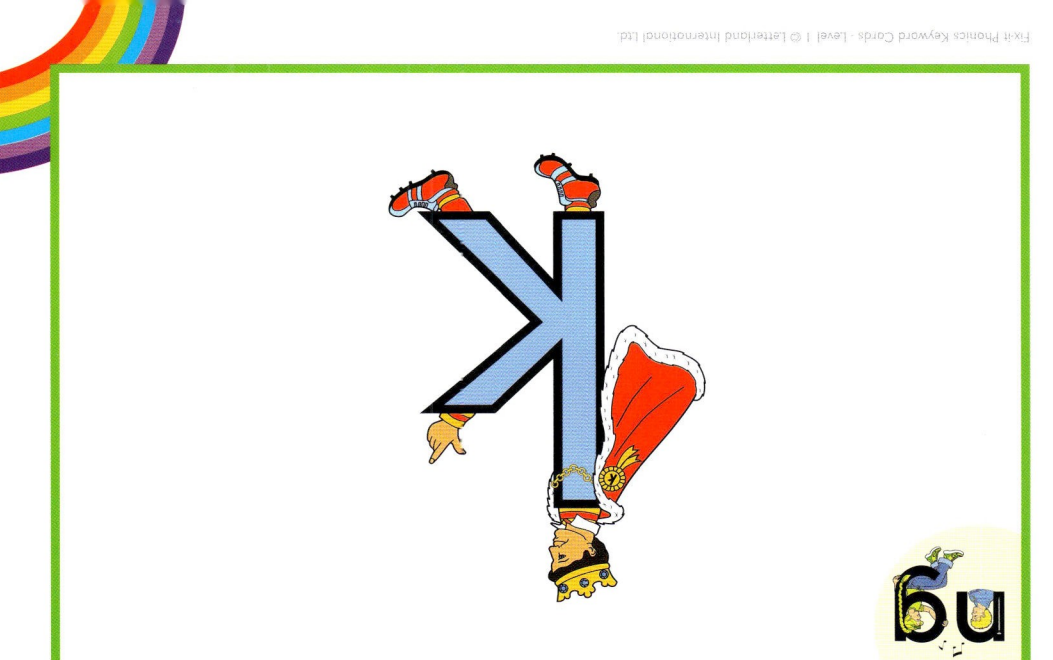
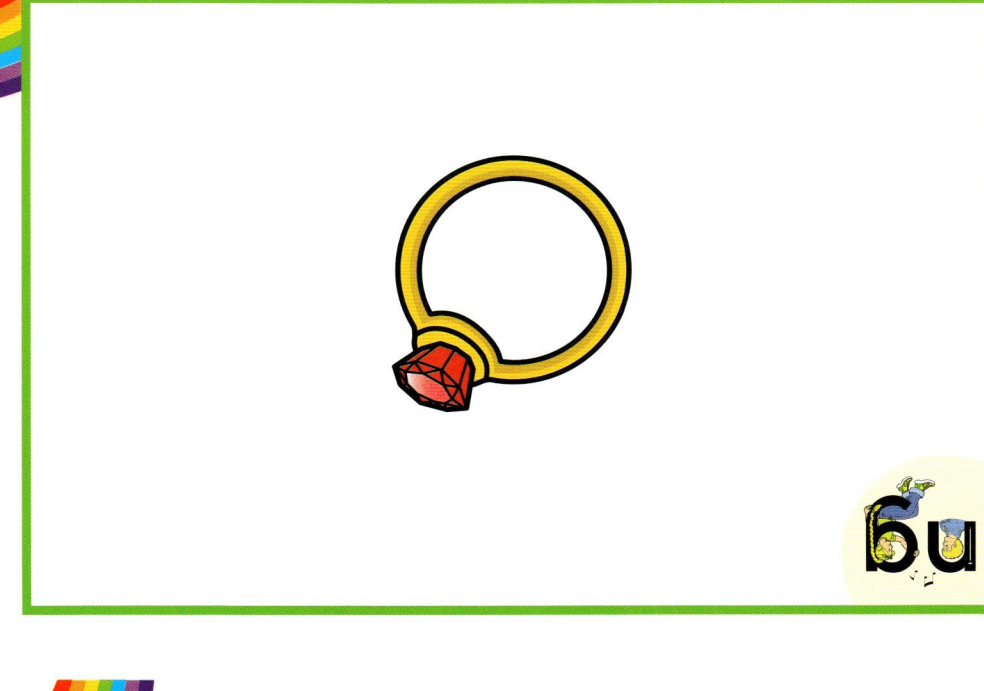

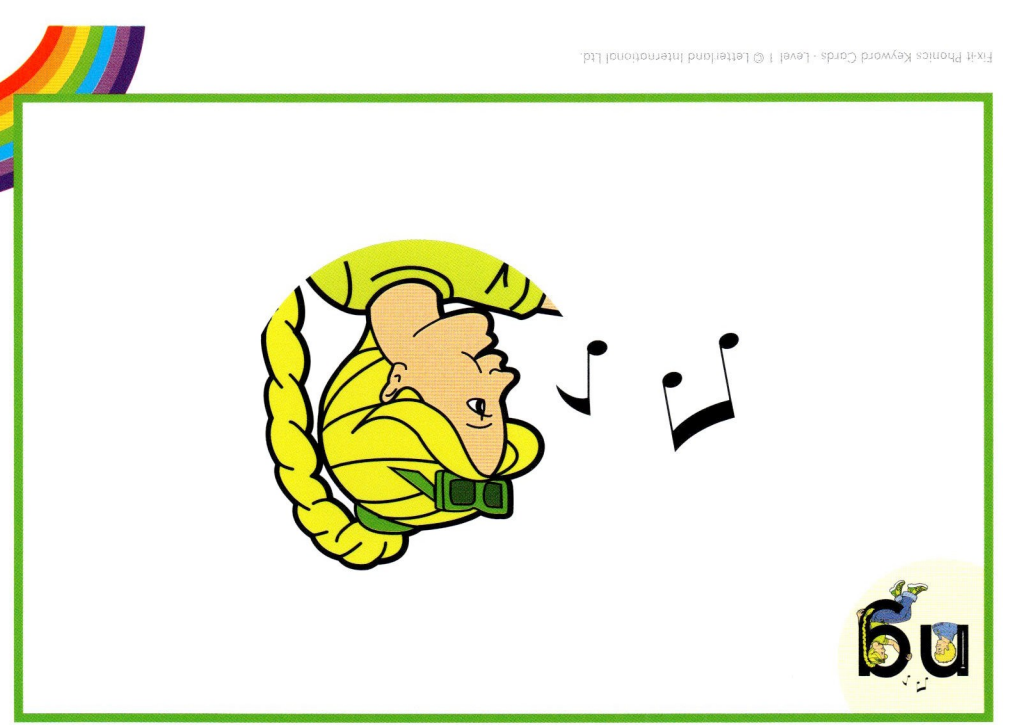

 sing

 quilt

 ring

 king

 alien

 apron

 eat

 acorn

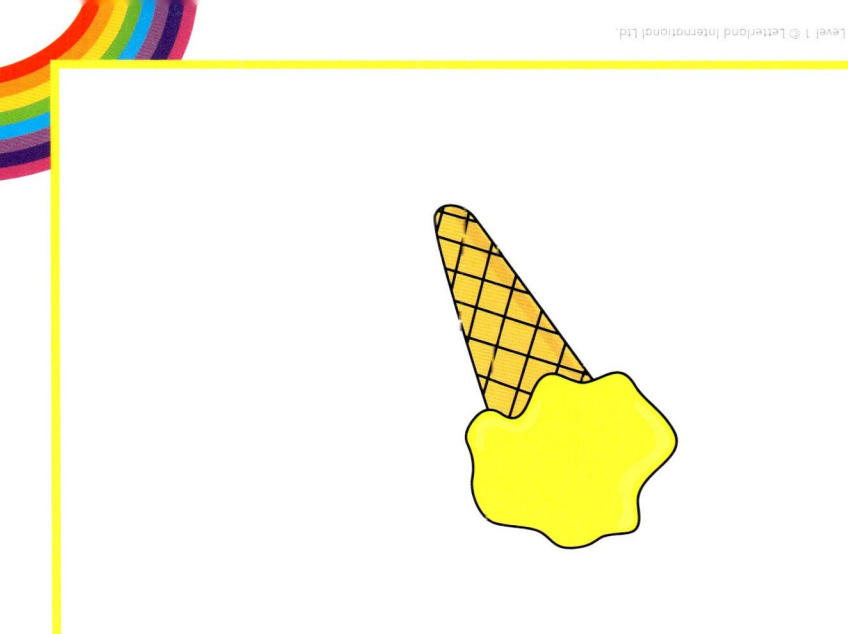

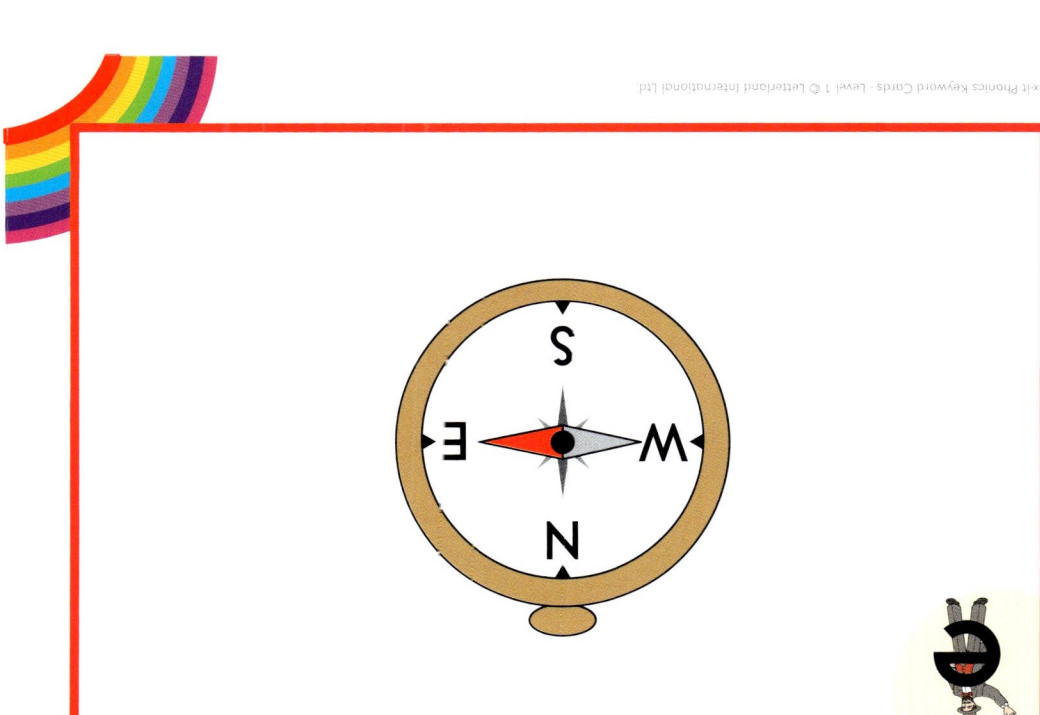

 eagle

 east

 island

 ice cream

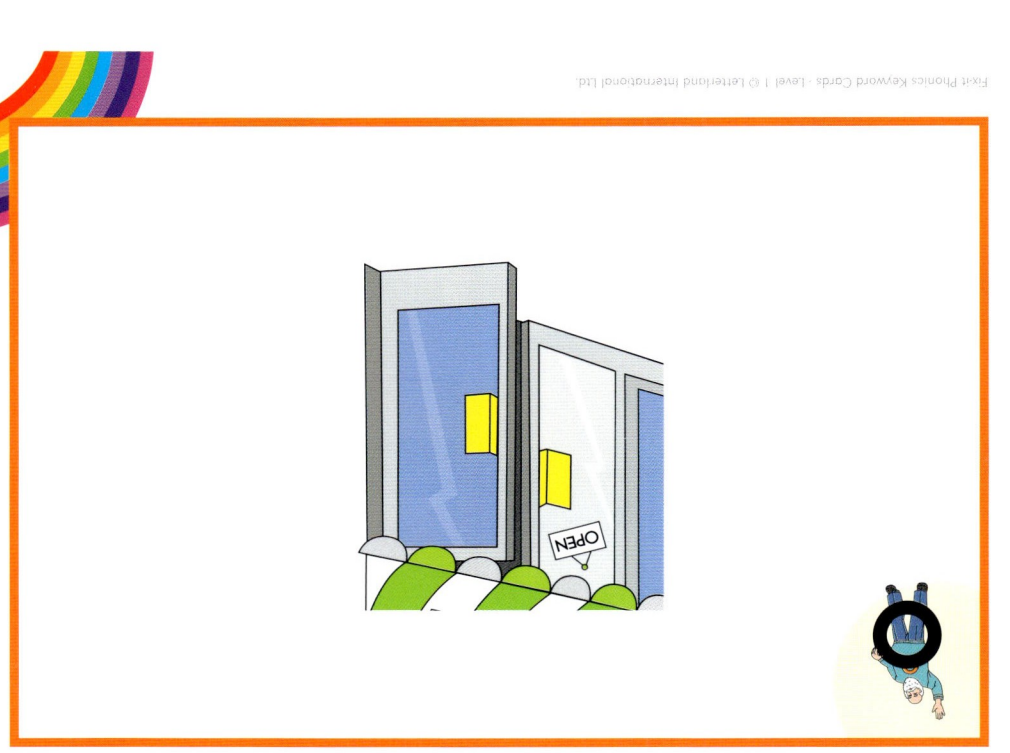
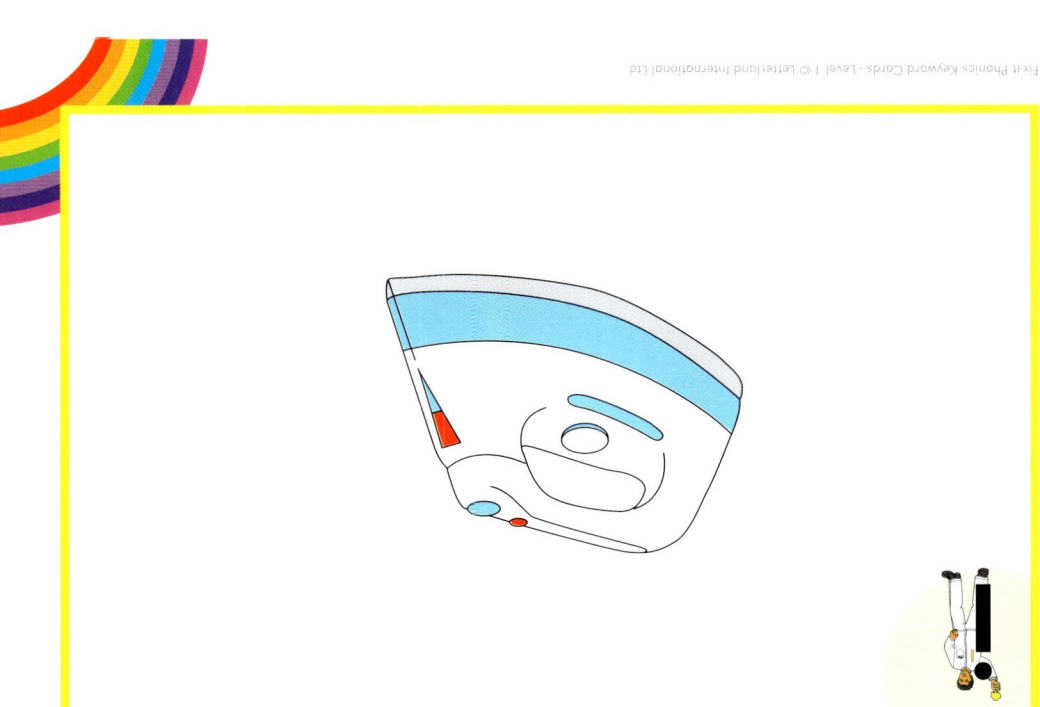

 open

 iron

 ocean

 old

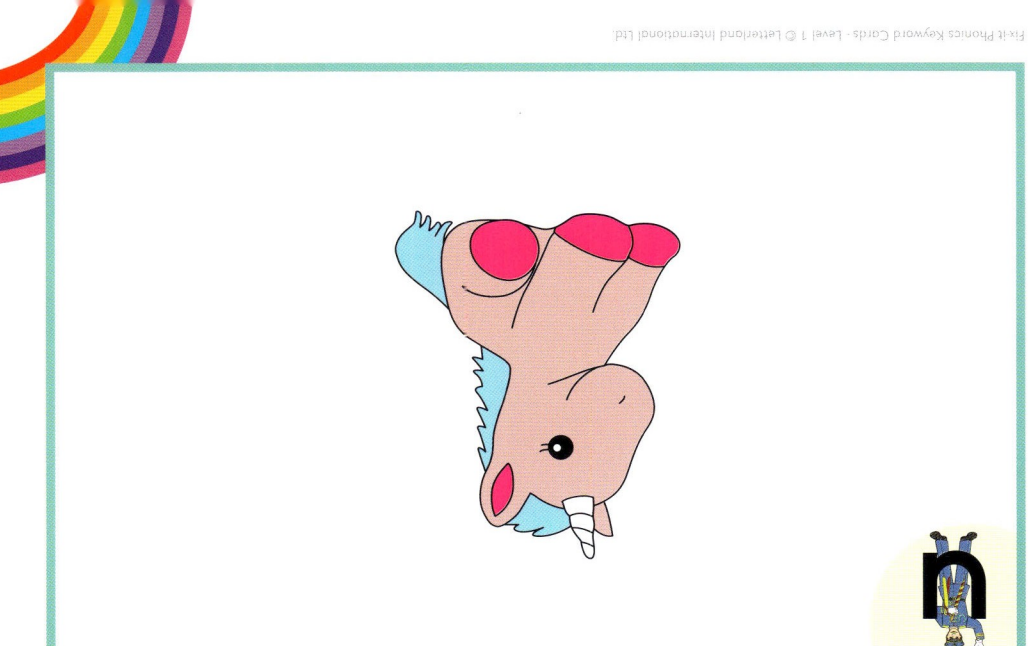

Make your own card

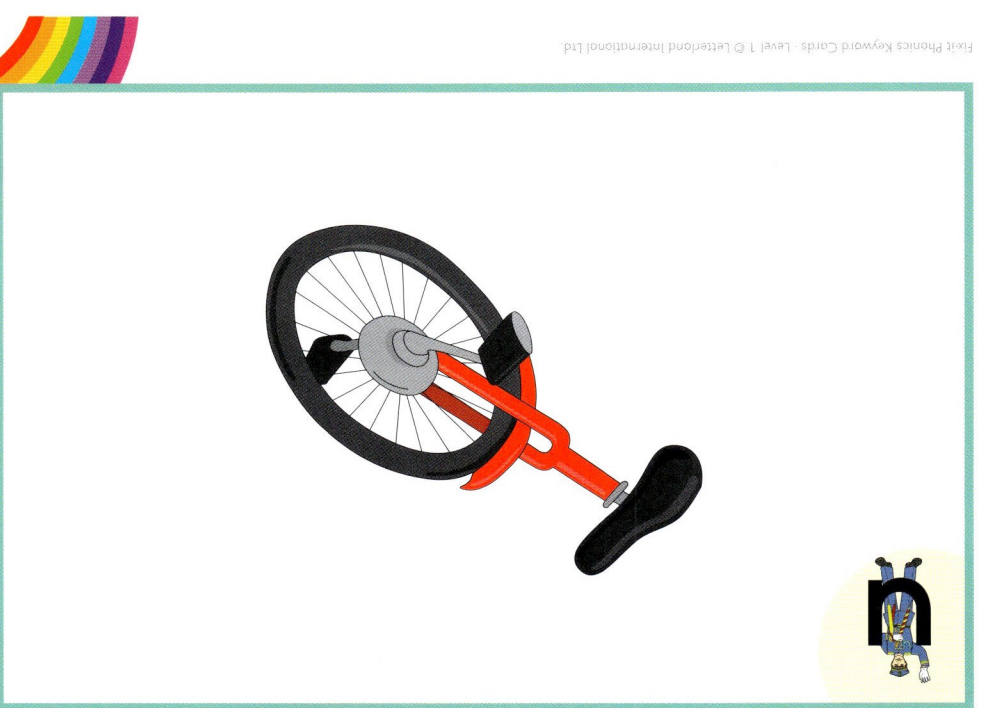

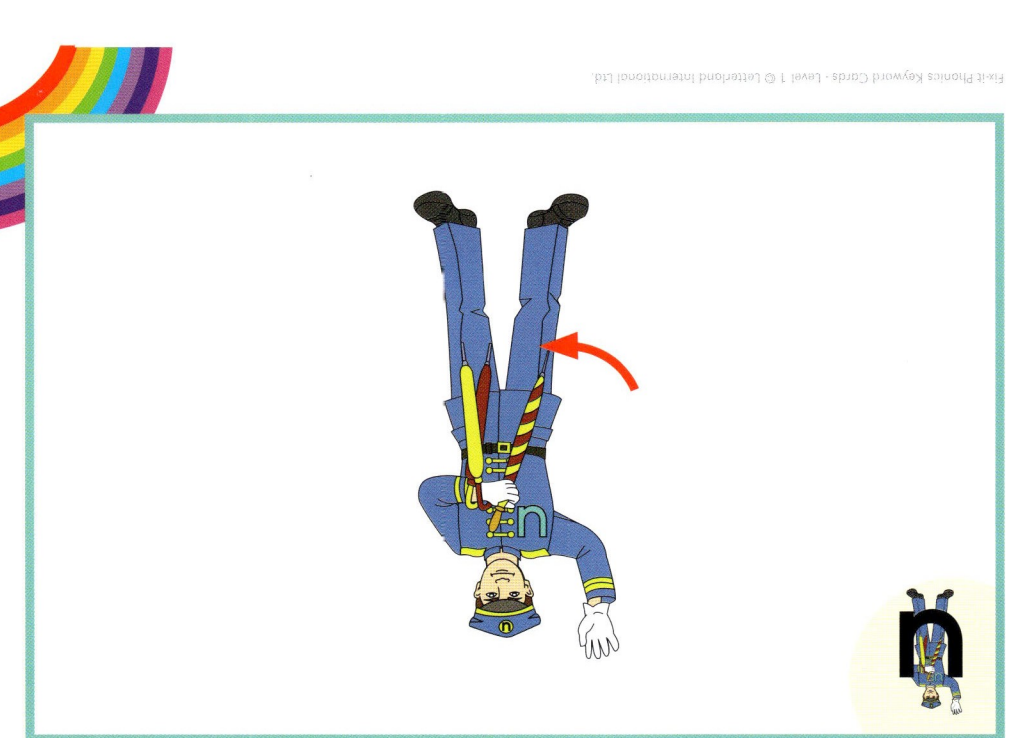

 unicycle

 uniform

Make your own card

 unicorn